Just when you think you are winning...
Humorous tales of a Hostage Negotiator

Text copyright © 2017 Martin D Richards

All Rights Reserved

Images copyright ©2017 James Lythe

All Rights Reserved

To my two children. An explanation of Dad's world and his sense of humour.

Contents

Contents 4
Introduction 5
Training 11
A cranes eye view 55
Batman on the Abbey 72
Burglar Bill and his mum 88
A desert drive to freedom 104
Gathering nuts in Kabul 121
A Happy Christmas in Iraq 144
Baby snatch tactics 163
Dog Day Afternoon in Starbucks 174
Britain's longest siege 198
Text on the move 218
Fish in a Barrel 230
No more mistakes and the final chapter? 244
Acknowledgements 250
About the Author 251

Introduction

'Are you ready to save a life?'

My ringing phone wakes me from my sleep. Blearily, I answer it only to hear the deep, Barry White-style voice of the Hostage Negotiator Coordinator coming through to me.

I was newly trained when I received that call. It was 2am, but the words I heard were enough to wake anyone up. The caller in question used the same phrase every time he rang. Perhaps it was his way of reminding us Police Negotiators of why it was that we were being telephoned in the middle of the night, reminding us of why we had to crawl out of our warm, cosy beds.

At home if I say the wrong thing my wife walks off in a huff and doesn't speak to me for a day. In this line of work, if I say the wrong thing someone dies. I can't tell you how conscious you become for the words coming out of your mouth. They say actions have consequences. Words do, ten-fold.

After receiving the briefing from the Negotiator coordinator on call, I take an Intelligence briefing. Afterwards I rapidly dress, drive into London and meet my team in yet another strange and depressing location which in those days before the use of Sat-Nav involved a heavy amount of map reading, getting lost and turning up late. Once there I'd stand for hours on end in pelting rain or freezing cold winds trying to convince a person I'd never met that their life was worth living. As work days go, it's something out of the ordinary.

Sometimes I was cancelled en route. I might have made it no further than cleaning my teeth or to the top of my drive, or the bottom of the M1 motorway before I'd receive a call saying that the incident had been brought to a close. Sometimes because they'd managed to convince the individual to get down. More often than not, because their attempts had been unsuccessful and used some form of force.

The family of Negotiators in the Metropolitan Police is made up of around 50 police officers. Once we're deployed to negotiate, the general set up used involves having three Negotiators on hand.

'Number One' Negotiator talks to the person having the crisis and is always the one in communication with them. 'Number Two' takes a more supportive role, which involves frantically scribbling notes and advising the 'Number One' on what *wonder phrases* to use next. You'll usually see them bent over pads of paper, scratching their heads and frowning like they're trying to write an essay on nuclear physics. 'Number Three's role is slightly different and involves logging a summary of the conversation that transpires between the Negotiator and the person they're talking to. They will be the 'runner', the go-between for the Negotiator and the Coordinator, updating them with the progress of the incident on a regular basis. The role of the 'Number Two', or 'Coach' as we call them, should never be underestimated. That person has the extra thinking time to reflect on and absorb the conversation taking place. One must never take that assimilation process for granted.

We negotiate in various ways. In person, up close, on the phone, through email, through social media. The person could be up a tree, on a crane, on a plane, on a roof. It pays to be flexible about your office space when it comes to this line of work. My preference when negotiating (like anyone else in this profession) is through a mobile phone, as it's the easiest way to build rapport and gain intelligence with the person with whom you're interacting. It's also a lot safer than face to face negotiation, particularly if the person you're dealing with is a bit of a live wire. The sort of person who douses themselves with petrol or arms themselves with a sword is not the sort of person you want to stand right next to and engage in conversation.

When you arrive on scene, the negotiating coordinator briefs you on the situation. During the time that you're en route they will have gained further intelligence from the scene commander and will be able to suggest a strategy to you.

After that we will conduct a risk assessment, which involves taking all sorts of safety measures into consideration. Should a certain footwear be worn? Is ballistic body armour required? For example, it's never a good idea to go up a tree wearing jeans, a t-shirt and slippery shoes to speak to a young man holding a loaded firearm to his head.

Some victims and offenders have a pre-conceived idea of what a police negotiator will be like, and it never helps if they've had some previous run-ins with the police that may have created some negative experiences. It can completely undo our work. (Try building rapport with someone who hates you before you've so much as opened your mouth. Believe me it's as hard as it sounds).

When we arrive the person in crisis is usually being spoken to by a uniformed officer. The handover stage from this officer to a Negotiator is very important. Sometimes the person being spoken to doesn't like the fact that the Negotiator is taking over, as they've built up a relationship with the officer at the scene already. They also like to have an element of control over who they speak to, and the unannounced arrival of a Negotiator makes them feel like they're no longer in charge. The operational reasons for switching Negotiators however far outweigh the negatives. As a tactical commander, you need to prove that you have deployed the best skills available to you at the moment that you needed them the most. Changing the local officer to a Negotiator also sends a message that we are treating the process seriously; that we *The Police*, are not going anywhere and that we are all in this for the long run.

The first introduction is always difficult.

'Hello, my name is Martin and I'm here to help' sounds a bit pathetic, but it's the clearest introduction that there is. If this gets no response, I usually follow up with a few sub-openers such as 'Help me understand what has brought you to this situation' or even 'I would really like to talk about what's going on with you, and that sword you're waving around is really getting in the way of that.' (Admittedly, I've only had to use that line three times, well four, if you count my two-year-old son running around dressed as a pirate).

Building instant rapport is never easy, yet it must be attempted to ensure that we have a chance to influence the person's behaviour during their crisis. Throughout this book I will detail my initial arrival at several incidents and you will begin to see what I mean: they're never easy and we must always prepare for the unexpected.

I became a Negotiator because I'd seen at first-hand how vital it was to gain trust when talking someone through a dangerous scenario and into safety. I was a young sergeant at a central London station when my colleague, a fellow sergeant on a late shift, had decided to post himself to the response vehicle answering 999 calls. Deep into their shift, a call was transmitted over the police radio that announced a determined man had climbed onto the roof of a BP petrol garage forecourt, near to the police station. He had doused himself in petrol and climbed onto the pump roof shelter and was shouting that he was ready to die. The crew of the response car, minus the sergeant who was nowhere to be found, were all in the station having their mid-shift refreshments. They dutifully downed their various eating utensils and rushed to the scene in the response vehicle. I decided to follow in the supervisor's car. We arrived together and what awaited us was astonishing. The missing sergeant was on the roof, in full uniform, doused in petrol and threatening to set himself on fire.

It's shocking when you see a colleague that you know and trust in such a situation. Thirty minutes earlier he was happily eating a sandwich and conversing with his colleagues! We all sort of shouted at him to see sense and that nothing can be so awful that you feel the need to set yourself on fire etc. It was at that point, right there and then that I thought to myself that I want that skill. I wanted that training, which would allow me to talk to someone who has turned themselves into an incendiary device and to bring them back to a state of calm. Needless to say, he did come down prior to any arrival of a negotiator that we thought we had better call. I don't think it was anything we said though. He was sent off for a psychiatric medical examination and returned to work a few weeks later. No one really spoke to him about what happened and no reason was ever given as to why he decided to do what he did on that day.

So why have I chosen now to write a book about my experience as a Hostage and Crisis Negotiator? Partly, because I know it touches on a subject we all understand. We all go through a crisis at some point in our lives.

When I talk to people about my job and this subject matter, they become intrigued, like it's some secretive, mystical occupation. But in truth, it's conversing with everyday people like you and me who have got themselves into an unhappy situation, for which we deploy a range of behavioural and persuasion techniques to enable them to adjust their thinking.

I don't profess to be the greatest Negotiator of all time because there are many of us out there and many who are far better and more experienced than I am. Thankfully though I've been presented with opportunities where I've been able to learn from the best, to pick up the odd word and sentence here and there and apply some good strategic insight. I've also been lucky enough to experience some amazing and dynamic incidents, which have immersed me into the most diverse range of emotions – be it sadness, excitement, fear or exhilaration. All of them have lived with me every day since they occurred.

It is often said that a Negotiator becomes one of the family. Not to sound too Tony Soprano about it, but you do become a close-knit community, sharing experiences and tribulations with others, who like you, are willing to pitch up at all hours in the pouring rain to save a life.

Training

When I achieved seventeen years' service, in the Metropolitan Police, I applied for and was selected to attend a two-week, intensive, negotiation course. In September 1998 I arrived at the Hendon Police College in North-West London, arriving on the Sunday night before the course began on the following Monday morning. The initial course meeting was held in a large room, with comfy chairs and unlimited supplies of tea, beer and biscuits, which was a promising start. The instructors briefly introduced themselves and told us that we were to watch a screening of *Dog Day Afternoon*, the famous Al Pacino film about a botched bank robbery where the perpetrators take hostages and attempt to negotiate their release. We were to examine the video and note down what we thought were the good and bad tactical decisions made by the law enforcement officers and to comment on the negotiation strategies used by a trained American Hostage Negotiator. All actors of course. 'Interesting start', I remember thinking, as my beer goggles kicked into action, 'beer and a 1970's film with a group of people I don't know. This is going to be a cushy course.' I couldn't have been more wrong.

At the start of our training on the following Monday morning, I took a moment to observe my fellow attendees. There are some in the police who we call 'Course Junkies.' These are the people who simply can't get enough of training courses. Not only that, but they spend *so* much of their time actually on training courses, that they're never at work for long enough to put all their training into practice. They're the people who like to adorn their office walls with certificates: from cycling proficiency and school swimming certificates to commendations from senior officers. The really serious collectors will invite you into their office for a meeting and sit you down. Then they ask you if you'd like a coffee, hoping you will say yes. They'll then leave you alone in their office for a few minutes whilst they go out to get said beverage. Leaving enough time in the interim to ensure that you've read their certificated walls and seen how wonderfully successful and well trained they are.

Then, there are other officers: those who know that the Negotiation Course is a good course and that it could further their career in one way or another but have no real intention of ever pursuing a career in negotiation. Why? For one thing, it's because they have absolutely no desire to be called away in the middle of the night in driving rain to solve a hostage situation. Some people like the comfort of their bed a little too much.

Then there are the rest of us: the ones who find it rewarding, worthwhile, exciting and interesting to learn new skills and are hungry to put them into practice.

Approximately twenty students from various UK police forces and departments will attend the course. There will also be a handful of international students, one of whom will invariably be from the FBI, our partner organisation in the field of negotiation. The FBI course will in turn receive one of our Negotiators as a reciprocal agreement, which ensures a nice blend of people and opinions from all sorts of backgrounds.

The course begins at 8.30 a.m. every morning and finishes with a debriefing and a quick drink at around 11 p.m. They are long, tiring and demanding days and each day follows a similar pattern. We listen to PowerPoint presentations from experienced instructors. We hear interesting guest speakers relay their stories and experiences. Then at the end of the day and into the evening, we participate in exercises that involve the filming and assessing of all the students on the course to see how they react to different scenarios. These scenarios will vary in intensity throughout the two weeks: from simple and calm suicide interventions, to knife wielding hostage incidents, where the student has to quell a person threatening to kill anyone and everyone within a ten-mile radius of where they're standing.

We are deployed in teams of three to five and watched over by the instructors who video our performances and then provide feedback.

All the course scenarios are acted out at the Metropolitan Police Detective Training School, or outside in the school grounds, often in view of new police recruits who are marching around the estate and doing their own training. They are often seen reporting fake motorists on our fake training roads for having no vehicle MOT, insurance certificate, or something else more sinister. These are the police recruits who will learn to alienate the driving public in years to come.

Watching them at work reminds me of the time I took my first student cop out on to the streets of London to guide and tutor.

The new recruits would complete their initial training, leave the police college and then be attached to a training team at the police station they had been posted to. The role of this training team was to hone this new officer's skills and give them a real flavour of what was to come. It was our chance to show them the real world of policing and encourage them to forget the naïve crap they learnt at Training School and what they knew about the job up until now. (Sounds a bit conceited I know).

In my first tutoring role I was out in the Mill Hill area of North-West London teaching this new cop, Chris, how to walk the beat, look important and convince the public he knew what he was doing. This often involved encouraging new officers to talk to the public and exercise their privileged powers in a gentle way. We usually started them off with asserting their new authority by stopping motorists for traffic offences. So, there we were, Chris and I walking along, with me teaching him to smile to the public and look less self-conscious. Suddenly I saw an open pickup truck driving by carrying Christmas trees. The rear, open section of the pickup was dropping chunks of wood and branches as it drove along the busy high street. In cop talk, this is what's known as an 'insecure load' (heinous crime that needs to be punished) and it requires a caution at least. I could see that cars were being forced to brake and swerve out of the way of the falling forest debris and I figured that this might be a good traffic offence for young Chris to pursue. So, I put my hand out to stop the van and directed Chris to go over to the driver and report him accordingly. No sooner had Chris stepped over to the vehicle however, did I see the driver swing the truck door open with a flourish, step out onto the pavement and come at Chris with an almighty fist and a torrent of verbal abuse. Looks like he was having a bad day and we were the last straw? Thankfully, good old Chris managed to get the upper hand just in time and managed, with my help, to detain the driver by forcing him to the ground. The drivers' behaviour was certainly unwarranted. Why, one might ask, would he act in this way, particularly over such a minor offence? It didn't take us long to find out. After a quick trip to the police station, we found out that this driver was in fact wanted for murder: a happy coincidence for which Chris was chuffed to take the credit. From here on, every time Chris and I went out to do the beat, I would see Chris nervous with anticipation, as if he assumed that every random motorist that we pulled over would jump out of his car and attempt to beat him to a bloody pulp. Chris later became a great friend and an incredibly enthusiastic, professional police officer. I like to think that it was all down to that first vehicle stop. First steps that remind you of just how important our job really is. Proper Christmas tree transportation is important after all.

Anyway. Let's get back to the Negotiators Training Course, where we were experiencing days packed full of exciting role plays and exhausting activities. It's hard to convey to someone who hasn't done this course just how stressful dealing with hostage situations every day for two weeks can be. I would go back to my room every night wondering if any of these incidents that we were presented with were actually real. Surely there can't be this many people out there who need this level of intervention and help? (How wrong I was). Occasionally, on the nights I slept during that course, I would fall asleep and dream of people jumping off ledges, overdosing on tablets, crying desperately to themselves or threatening to kill a hostage.

Sleeping at Hendon Training School for that two-week period reminded me of a time earlier in my career when I had been employed as a Recruit Instructor at the Police Training College. My role was to train brand new recruits and turn them into cops, which sounds easy and fun in theory but in reality it is not a cushy job. One Monday morning, a student was sent (not by me) to his room for failing to shave for the morning parade. A heinous offence in police training circles! That same recruit, later that morning, failed to turn up for his first class. Consequently, the instructor sent another student to try and locate him. There was no answer from his room after knocking on the door. After an hour of his fellow classmates searching public areas, people began to get concerned. By morning coffee time he still hadn't been located, until one sharp-eyed recruit spotted him standing on the 14th floor ledge of the accommodation block!

Instructors were urgently called to the location and his door was immediately kicked open by one of them, so we could enter and reach his window and talk to him from his room. Not happy with this intervention, he walked around the narrow ledge that hugged the building and repeatedly threatened to jump and claimed that the studying and discipline of police schooling was just too much for him (really?). As the schools' crisis management protocol dictated, the local police were called and soon after the Negotiators attended. One of the student's demands (whilst up there, circling the ledge) was for more study time and less shaving. Never going to happen, I thought, we need to manage his expectations. This was the Metropolitan Police after all and we had high standards to maintain. If he wanted more study time and less nit-picking on house rules, he should have had the foresight to join the Devon and Cornwall Constabulary. (Inside joke here). After another hour of circling and whining, the chap decided to come down and after a brief discussion with his Instructor's Team Leader he came to the decision that a career in the police probably wasn't for him.

You do get recruits like this sometimes. One cut his wrists after being sent to his room to press his trousers. We all hate ironing, but that's an extreme reaction by anyone's standards. After several suicide attempts made by students, a crisis meeting was held by the Senior Management Team to examine whether our training techniques were too intense or our discipline system too rigid. The answer was…'no' and 'no', so we carried on as normal. From a member of the public's perspective this may sound harsh, but I'm pretty sure the general public don't want to be surrounded by untidy police officers with scraggly beards, no creases in their trousers and no knowledge of the rules. (Although some of the officers I see walking the streets of London nowadays do seem to fit into that category). Anyway. Back to the Negotiators Course.

Throughout the two weeks we were graded on our performance and given an assessment score. If you reached a certain score, you were viable to become a Negotiator. It was during the course introductions however that I realised my opening pitch – 'Hello, my name is Martin Richards and I am a firearms team leader in SO19' - was in for some serious competition. There were the usual sergeants there with mundane jobs from around the country, with zingy openers like 'Hello, my name's Jim, I work in fraud in Dorset', alongside the more exotic tactical commanders, who had openers like 'Hi, I'm Special Agent Pete Thundercloud, FBI.' It's hard to beat that! If I was keeping hostages behind a barricade and I heard that introduction from outside the stronghold, I'd probably just walk out with my hands held high. On top of that cool name, the man had a voice like honey that would trick you into saying 'yes' to his every command. It was like he was some sort of Jedi walking amongst civilians, trained by Yoda and adept in all the aspects of which we had yet to skim the surface. He knew what you were thinking before you did. (The Force was very strong in that one. So much so, he ended up marrying one of the other students on the course. A Jedi mind trick if ever I saw one).

One element of the course that really struck a chord with me was when one of the instructors spoke to us about how we were going to have to deal with the opposing party trying to 'win' the conversation. Occasionally when you're negotiating, you come up against people who only want to insult you and try to play you at a reactionary level.

To remedy this, the instructor asked us to remember a time when something that someone had said to us had got us hot under the collar, and we had ended up reacting in the wrong way. That was an easy one for me: being in the police means that you become hardened and desensitised to members of the public calling you nasty things and spitting in your face, but on one occasion, a member of the public had crossed my personal line. At this particular stage in my career I weighed twelve stone and considered myself fairly slim, but when I was wearing body armour under a coat and a reflective jacket over the top, I looked very large. During one tour of duty, I was standing outside the Houses of Parliament overlooking a demonstration, when a yob came up to me, out of nowhere, and shouted *'you fat bastard'* right into my face. It was the only time I had ever been called fat and it was the only time in my whole career that I'd become upset and angry about a comment made by a member of the public. What does that say about my body image?

The instructor asked us to re-tale these experiences to the group. Other examples from the class were, a wife having a go at one of the guy's home cooked dishes, a mother picking on their facial hair, and the common one, having a go at someone's driving ability.

Once we'd aired our individual moments of ill temper, the instructor informed us that no matter what the situation we were faced with, we were never to argue with the person we were negotiating with. No matter how provocative they became, we were to keep our temper and do everything within our power to calmly and quietly defuse the situation. Sometimes, he said, this would mean having to stand and listen to a lot of threats and insults. In this instance, you were to remain impassive and not let your true feelings show. After all, if the other person were to sense a weakness in us, they could exploit it. 'Look,' he said, 'I'll show you.' He dragged some unfortunate 'volunteer' from our group and proceeded to humiliate him in front of us, pointing out things about his hair and dress sense – or lack of both. Of course we all laughed, relieved that it wasn't us at the front of the class. But then he said, 'Right, let's turn the tables: it's your turn.' The victim – who by this point was scarlet with rage and close to tears then started to give the instructor some critical feedback of his own. The instructor just stood there, smiling benignly, accepting every barbed comment and insult.

As an experienced cop who has frequently been on the receiving end of such barrages, I do genuinely believe that adopting this sort of non-emotional resistance is a skill that can only come from experience. I find it always helps to expose yourself to situations where you can put this negative experience into real practice. Being in a difficult marriage is, I find one such example of an effective learning environment.

The first time I actually attempted to talk to someone in a crisis after this course was a moment I'll never forget. My heart leapt from my chest, my mouth went dry and my legs felt weak. Then my training kicked in, I engaged my active listening skills and began looking for hooks in what the person was saying.

The first scenario on the actual course was not as successful. In fact the training never appeared at all, let alone 'kick in.' It was a domestic incident between a man and his wife. He had barricaded them both into their house, probably because she'd burnt his toast or stopped giving him blow jobs after they were married, and so barricading her into the house had probably seemed like the only sensible means of remedying this.

The instructor had split the class into two in order to decrease the ratio of students to instructors, which made for a more accurate student assessment. I walked up to a closed door with half the class watching me. The instructors held their clipboards to their chests and stared at my every move like hawks. Body language is a highly important factor in these tasks, and they wanted to see how I placed myself, how I walked, whether I exuded confidence in the situation, (I guessed I didn't). The moment dripped with suspense, like something out of an action film. All that was missing was dynamic background music and a bucket of popcorn.

I approached the door, a hundred thoughts whirring through my head. What was my next move? Should I knock? Perhaps I shouldn't. The last thing I wanted was for the husband to open the door. I didn't have any body armour on and if he rushed at me with a knife, HI was a goner. I knew that my first step was to try and build rapport with the enraged husband. But how do you build rapport through a closed door? In the end, I decided not to open the door and instead open my mouth. I shouted, 'My name is Martin and I am here to help.' I paused. What next? Perhaps if I summoned all the knowledge I'd gathered from my last three days of training, I could create a suitably eloquent and commanding second sentence that would compel this infuriated person to come out of his house, so I could rescue his wife and become a hero.

In my mind, I press fast forward and the instructor, debriefing the class, is saying 'That's how you do it, well done Martin.' I thought long and hard. I needed to get this guy to soften. Maybe I could talk about the good times he and his wife had shared in their relationship and get him to think about what the future might hold. Sure, there might be certain compromises along the way, but barricading your loved one in the house doesn't need to be the answer. Maybe I should try and understand what had caused this man to flip out in the first place. Maybe I should encourage him to redirect his attention towards a new hobby or life skill. In the end I decided on... 'Please could you come out.' I waited. After a moment a male voice called back, 'Why?' That one shocked me. I wasn't prepared for it. What was I meant to say in reply? 'Because I want you to' didn't hold much weight, but I went with it anyway. The voice replied, 'No.' 'Please?' I said. 'No,' he said. And on it went. Not quite the draw dropping perfectionism I was hoping for.

As the conversation went on, things improved (slightly). The instructors started to tone down the role play, probably because it was my first attempt and they all felt sorry for me and partly (probably) they didn't want to bore the rest of the class who were having to listen to this circular and rubbish conversation.

Reflecting back on this role play, I was prompted some years back to buy an old VCR player on eBay and to dig out my worn VHS tape of negotiating exercises I participated in on this course. At the start of writing this book, I transcribed the exercise conversations from the first week of this course to give you readers some insight into just how painful my first experience was.

It was rather unpleasant, listening and watching me (with a full head of hair) and seeing just how nervous I really was.

The role players were all very experienced (they knew how to tie us into knots, chew us up, and spit us out). They were better at active listening than we were and consequently they were tough people to deal with. That said, if you can negotiate with a Negotiator, everyone else is easy. At least, that's the theory. All the scenarios we were given were based on real events. My first exercise was situated in a news agent where an armed robbery had gone wrong and the gunman was held up in a store room with two hostages. The two hostages were called Mr and Mrs

Brownlow, the shop owners. We had formed a negotiating cell in the shop and were to talk with the assailant by means of an intercom. In reality we were in adjoining rooms on the first floor of the Detective Training School at Hendon. Next door to us down the corridor were the assessors, who were watching me via a group of monitors and compiling a marking guide. These guides used headings such as team work, resilience, active listening, temperament and operational awareness. The role players were trained to use your words and twist them against you, thus rendering you powerless and a bit foolish in the process. So here I was. Week one. First assessment and quite honestly rubbish.

Our initial brief contained the scenario background as mentioned above. Midway through the conversation, the suspect requests a car to leave the scene. I press the intercom and a gruff voice answers.

M. Hello my name is Martin, I am here to help. What do you want the car for?

S. To leave.

Obviously.

M. What's actually been going on then?

S. A bit of an argument. It's all sorted now so get me a car and I can leave.

M. Tell me what's actually happened? Help me to understand why you want to leave there.

S. Look one minute you want to help me the next minute you're not. Just get me a car.

M. I do want to help you and see what I can do for the vehicle but that's going to take a bit of time. While we are waiting for the car, I want you to tell me what's going on.

Four sentences in and my first cock up. He'll now think a car will be coming to him. Maybe I will get away with the 'while we are waiting for the car' statement.

S. So I'm getting a car then. Thanks.

Shit. Seems like I didn't get away with it.

M. I said we will try and see what we can do about that.

S. You said you were waiting for the car, make your mind up.

M. Listen we are all part of a team here. I have heard your request and it's going to be considered.

S. You said I could have a car just now.

See, told you. He won't let it go now. Fucking role players.

S. Listen how did you get down here? You came in a car, didn't you?

M. Well... yes.

S. Then you don't need to get one. You have a car here. Just leave the keys by the door and we will go away, problem solved.

At this point I should really have told him that he won't be leaving to go anywhere. He has committed an armed robbery and taken two hostages after all. But for some bizarre reason, unbeknownst to me, I fail to communicate this particular piece of information, which gets me into about twenty minutes of trouble, as you will now see.

M. It's not me that makes decisions here, it's a team decision.

This is actually true, but never really convincing and frustrates the hell out of criminals. They always want to speak with the person in charge and we never let them. The reason for this is partly because it builds in a buffer and takes the pressure off us. If we can't make decisions, then we can't be forced too. A bit like a car salesman who goes in to see his boss to 'see what he can do for you.' It also allows us to build in delays which buys us time to obtain information and build rapport with the person we are negotiating with.

S. Then let me speak with the person that makes the decisions. Am I speaking to the monkey then, rather than the organ grinder?

Standard response from a suspect and quite reasonable really.

M. Well we all make decisions and I'm part of the decision-making process.

Shit! Now I have said that I make decisions.

S. Then maybe you can be part of the team that makes decisions to leave the keys outside the door. I heard of police not making decisions, but you have a committee to make a decision on leaving some keys. What rank are you?

M. We are all the same rank, it's a decision-making process in order to make a decision, I am an Inspector.

God now I am struggling, a decision-making process in order to make a decision? WHAT AM I SAYING? I don't think anyone in the history of the universe has ever used the word 'decision' so many times in one sentence.

S. So you are in charge of lots of people and can't make a decision about some fucking keys?

Yes, it does sound weird when you put it like that.

M. Like I say I have heard your request and it will be considered by a lot of people because obviously something has gone on inside. It's a decision. A team decision.

Dear God man stop saying the word decision!

M. Listen, I don't know who you are and if I am going to give anything anywhere, I need to know who I am dealing with.

Now I sound angry.

He hangs up.

We have a team discussion. We agree to say that we have passed the request on and to focus attention on who is in there with the criminal and what exactly has been happening. (Which is easier said than done with this role player, who I am sure will deviate repeatedly, asking questions about the car model being sent to him, the style of keys and whether it has reverse parking until I give up and burst into tears).

M. Hello, it's Martin again. I have good news!

S. Yeah go on.

M. Who are you again? I have been asked to speak to you by intercom, so I would like to know I'm talking to the same person

S. Don't worry about who I am, you can call me 'Sir' I like the idea of someone calling me Sir, especially a police Inspector.

M. OK Sir.

Now I sound sarcastic.

M. The good news is that your request has been passed on and is being seriously considered.

S. That's good news is it?

I must admit that's what I would think. I don't know why I said it was 'good news.' It's barely even 'news.' Yet I persevere and try to persuade him into thinking that it really is 'good news.'

M. It's good news in that it's being seriously considered. The request is being dealt with seriously and the decision-making process has been taken away from the room. And as soon as I have information about the vehicle, I will come straight back to you.

S. I will assist you with your decision making and speed things up a bit and tell you that unless I get this car and the keys by seven o'clock you are going to be very sorry.

M. What do you mean by sorry?

S. Wait and see.

M. How many people are there in there with you? I need to know that everyone in there is OK.

S. Listen we have just had an argument it's all OK now.

M. Who with? (Silence)

B. *Hello?* (Different voice)

M. Hello who is this?

B. Mr Brownlow, who are you?

M. My name is Martin. I work with the police and there are lots of police out here worried about you and Mrs Brownlow, is she OK?

B. Yeah she's OK we are both OK. We just had an argument, it's all sorted now and he just wants a car. Can you let him have a car? You said it was OK earlier so give him it and he will leave us alone.

M. I don't know if you heard me say earlier that's its being dealt with very seriously. These decisions take time. What's your first name sir?

B. Roger.

M. Roger, these things take time. There are a lot of people out here trying to resolve this. We want everyone to come out of there safely. Can I speak with Bridget, your wife?

S. (Shouting) Now, look it's not one of those fucking coffee mornings you know, I want the car and some keys!

M. I know, I know, look can you give me your first name?

S. I told you, you can call me sir.

M. Like I said, that decision is being taken by people outside of this room. Now as soon as I get some positive information, I will come back to you with it. I want to know in the meantime what's been going on. If you come out and talk to me it will be a lot easier than talking on this intercom.

We are taught to ask someone to come out of a stronghold from the onset. It's wishful thinking, but then again if you don't ask you don't get.

S. Look, I tell you what's going to happen. I don't want to talk to you until the car keys are sorted out. (Hangs up).

Another team discussion follows. There are three strategies for us to consider. One: ask him to release Bridget as she's done nothing wrong. Two: give him a reality check and tell him that the police have seen him with a gun and that he won't be allowed to leave. Three: go the long way round and ask him lots of questions. Questions about the car, where he plans to go, how much petrol he thinks he'll need. I personally like the 'bring him to reality' strategy, so we decide to make a play for it and I press the intercom again.

S. Hello, have you got this car yet?

M. No, as I said these things take time. What sort of car did you want anyway?

S. One with four wheels and an engine.

Hilarious

M. I also want to know where you think you are going to go?

My colleague (who is actually my coach) whispers this last question to me. A whisper that our dear old criminal suspect seems to pick up on.

S. Who's that with you?

Shit.

M. This is Hilary.

S. Is she one of those decision-making people?

M. No, she is just helping me. Now let me tell you what we think has gone on from our end. You have been seen with a gun and have taken Bridget and Roger into a stock room against their wishes. Now that's the information from our end. I would like to know from your end whether or not that is in fact true or whether there is something else that has gone on that we don't know about from our end.

About time. I should have said this ages ago. Perhaps minus a few 'ends.'

S. You been told a load of porkies mate. There are no guns in here. You have spoken to Roger. He is fine. He didn't mention a gun, did he? We just want to go home.

M. That's the information we have from a police officer. But I want to know from your end what has actually happened. Because that's what maybe not happened from your end.

Too many 'ends.'

S. Rubbish, had an argument and now it's all sorted, no guns in here.

M. We have been speaking to you via this intercom and the reception isn't very good. If we can get a phone in to you it would be easier.

S. Can you speak up I can't hear you, this intercom is rubbish.

Arsehole.

M. Then allow us to get a phone in. You have been moaning that at your end you can't hear very well.

Stop saying 'ends', Martin!

S. So you can get me a telephone, but not a set of keys?

M. Well the phone is very handy whereas a car isn't.

What am I actually saying! Seriously?

S. The car is handy. You came down in a car, you told me that.

M. The decision on whether or not to give you a car hasn't been made. I can make the decision on the phone because I have it here.

Dammit I shouldn't have said that. I know what he'll say next.

S. Oh so you can make some decisions, but not others?

Yup...knew it.

M. Right... er...no...er...

29

S. Is that what you are saying?

M. No...er... the car is an important decision... because the information we had...about a firearm.

Help me, please!

S. I don't think I can trust you. For a simple request like getting a set of keys you have to form a committee and pass things on and the minute you want a telephone in here to make things easier for *you*, you can make decision.

M. But the car will take time.

S. The car won't take time. You parked one outside you can place the keys by the door.

Oh fuck of!

M. Going back to what has happened-

S. Answer the question! Stop changing the subject. Get that woman Hilary who is with you to bring the keys to the door.

M. I need Hilary in here with me.

S. How many are there of you?

M. Three of us.

S. Three of you, and none of you can make decisions. And this job is so important that not one of you can bring the keys to the door?

M. This job is very important. We are worried about the people in there with you.

S. Get Hilary who keeps bloody whispering to you to bring the keys. Mrs Brownlow wants a glass of water. It's getting very hot in here.

M. I can do that.

S. Oh so you can get phones and water but not keys.

He hangs up on me again.

We have another team discussion. Before the exercise began, we were given a deadline of 7pm to solve it. That deadline is now thirty seconds away. We are taught to always talk through a deadline, at the very least have him on the phone talking to us rather than carrying out some threat. I hastily press the intercom again.

M. Hello, is everyone OK in there?

S. Have you got the fucking keys? I asked for these 15 minutes ago. I am getting serious pissed off!

Shit, now he's angry.

M. Yes, you sound angry and I do appreciate that you are angry.

Why do I speak this rubbish?

S. You sound like a pompous arrogant little shit who doesn't care about me. I will show you. Give me the fucking keys!

Suddenly we hear sounds of a female screaming, followed by the sounds of slapping and punching. A female voice cries out 'Help!'

At this point we were taught to challenge the violence, be firm and ask the suspect to desist.

M. Stop that, don't do that, don't do it!

I am really shouting now.

There then follows a period of time where I'm pressing the intercom asking if everything is okay and telling the Suspect that I'm worried whilst he yells abuse at me. Things are not going well, and people are getting hurt.

We decide to leave him alone for a bit to calm down.

A few minutes go by and our next strategy is to impress on him a reality check, in that we need to establish that no one has a gun on the premises. We press the intercom again. This time a woman's voice answers.

B. Hello is this Martin? I am ever so worried...

M. Hello is this Bridget?

Suddenly the suspect comes back on the phone.

S. What the fuck is going on? Who said you could talk to her?

I hear what sounds like a very angry suspect snatching the phone from Bridget.

M. In relation to the vehicle.

S. In relation to the vehicle?

M. Like I said to you, what we know from your end, or our end, is that there is somebody in there with a gun. Now the decision-making process is taking some time because they can't allow someone to leave that premises if they have a firearm. Now you must be able to appreciate that.

S. *(shouting)* Well because you can't make a fucking decision, Roger has had a bit of a slap and if you don't get the keys in here soon it will be more than a slap. It is all down to you mate because you can't make a decision.

M. Injuring people and slapping around people is not going to help your cause is it?

S. It's making me feel much better though.

M. But it's not going to help you.

S. Get me the keys and fuck off!

He hangs up on me again. I press the intercom.

M. Look, I wanted to know if Roger requires any first aid.

S. Look, he is OK now, but he will get more of a slap if I don't get the keys.

This is beginning to feel like Groundhog Day.

M. Further injuring people will not help you. Help me to understand-

He hangs up again.

And that's my 25 minutes of fame. Afterwards, we all change roles with Hilary taking my position and me taking hers before we receive a summary of feedback which, I think it's safe to say, won't be too shining on my part.

Experience and hindsight are a marvellous thing. When I look back at this tape, I realise that I was too timid in my approach. When dealing with this type of incident it is often clear as day to the person we are talking to, that he or she is not going to be permitted to just drive off into the sunset. They have committed a serious crime and they know it. An early reality check and an assertive attitude from us is required at the outset. We can offer them legal advice, remind them that any further acts of violence or the commission of additional crimes will be unhelpful to them. We can be honest about what will happen should they surrender. Often in these situations the person is too emotional and irrational to think clearly. Our job is to enable them to think clearly by explaining the benefits of a safe surrender. Before we do this however, it's important to deal with the emotions so that the person can listen and understand the rationales we are presenting. During this particular incident I was so afraid of saying the wrong thing and of upsetting the armed suspect that I failed to take appropriate control. My language was repetitive and full of police speak, continued use of the phrase 'decision making process' being one such example. Still, it was my first attempt. As I recall, four other colleagues spoke with the suspect and he eventually released Mr and Mrs Brownlow before surrendering to armed police. The main role player of the Suspect was a detective superintendent in the Met Police who looked nothing like his menacing voice. He played the role and me, so well that, nice guy as he was, I was never able to like him when we did eventually meet.

Days pass and I have several other attempts in convincing people in a crisis to do as I request and change their behaviour. This following example was week two of the course and a slightly improved performance. Although not entirely polished as you will see.

This role play was situated inside a doctor's surgery where Rose, a suicidal and revengeful mother, was threatening to set fire to the place after having taken a doctor hostage. His name was Alfred Jack who was employed at the surgery in question. She had also poured petrol all over the floor and furniture. We had been there for about an hour and a half and I was the third person to speak to Rose. I was crouched behind a long shield with my other team members. Rose wanted some coffee about an hour into the incident. The commander agreed with this request and a delivery plan was created. Armed officers delivered the coffee to the entrance and left it for Rose to collect. Whilst we changed the team roles, we decided to allow her some time and space to drink the coffee and reflect on our previous discussions.

Every item delivered to the person we are in dialogue with needs a carefully thought out and a precise delivery plan must be written. The plan needs to be read out to the person, so they understand fully what is going to happen and what we expect them to do. Included within these plans are what the delivery team will be dressed in, how many will be part of the delivery team, the route they will take to arrive at the premises, the method of transport they will use and what they will be carrying the requested object in. This may sound very detailed to you the reader, but it is necessary so that we can ensure there are no surprises that could lead to misunderstandings and/or reckless action. We may also need to outline our rationale for sending a team of armed officers that look like Robo Cop rather than PC plod wearing reflective jackets and a rather unfortunate looking tit shaped helmet.

Talking of delivery plans, I remember that on one training exercise during the course, we were sent to Heathrow airport to deal with a make-believe terrorist that had hijacked a plane. During negotiations, the decision was taken to deliver a field phone into the aircraft. A field phone is a phone with a wire attached to it, which makes it easier for us to communicate with the offender as it's a dedicated line with a good reception. The firearms team decided that it was too risky to walk across an open field to the plane, so they devised an idea where a specially trained police dog would deliver the phone with it strapped to its back. We prepared the delivery. The phone was secured by means of a harness to the dog's back. The dog was fully briefed as to its task. (What it was told by the handler I hasten to think. 'Right Fido, walk up to the plane with this phone, hand it to the nasty terrorists and leg it back before you are shot, got it?' 'Woof'). The briefing ended and Fido tottered off towards Flight 347 to Tenerife. He looked, in my expert opinion, slightly nervous. So far so good. That is until he got halfway across the field and the phone fell off into a muddy puddle. I remember seeing the dog look confused and stop in his tracks, looking back to the red-faced handler and back to the plane, unsure of what his next step in life should be. Keeping true to the briefing he'd received earlier, he carried on to the plane. You can imagine the surprise Mr Terrorist must have had, when having been promised a phone, he was presented with a panting and slightly confused looking dog at the first-class cabin door. We had been speaking to him through an Arabic interpreter and he might have thought that we had said dog, not phone. Needless to say, he wasn't very happy and he shot a make-believe hostage to teach us a lesson. The dog then proceeded to walk around for an hour looking confused and relieved itself against one of the front tyres. We never attempted *that* delivery technique again.

Anyway, let's get back to suicidal Rose, who was just finishing up her coffee so now seemed like a great time to chat. My colleagues who had been speaking to her previously had established that she had blamed one of the doctors based at the surgery for the death of her son, Phillip, who had committed suicide by hanging himself. The doctor had missed the depression signs and failed to prescribe medication that, according to Rose, would have helped her son and prevented this tragedy. Now it was my turn to talk to her.

M. Hello Rose. You won't recognise my voice. My name is Martin and I am part of the team that has been talking to you.

R. What do you want?

M. Are you ready to talk again, Rose? I hope you enjoyed your coffee.

R. It was fine.

M. Did Alfred get a cup? (Alfred or Doctor Jack was the name of the doctor that she had taken hostage).

R. Yes.

M. Listen, firstly I want to say thank you for sticking to the plan, obviously it's a very dangerous time, us delivering coffee. We are very grateful that you did as you were asked.

Now when I said this, I did mean that it was dangerous delivering this particular cup of coffee in this particular scenario: there was a gun present and petrol poured all over the place. I did not mean that delivery of coffee was, per se, dangerous, though the comment caused much merriment amongst my fellow team members who decided to bring me a cup of coffee after the debrief dressed in fire retardant gauntlets. You can't beat police humour.

R. Look just talk to Doctor Jack. He has woken up now.

This is the poor man she was keeping hostage and clearly so bored with events he can take a short nap.

M. (*I call out*) Alfred, can you hear me...?

A. (*Alfred replies*) Hello.

M. Hello Alfred. My name is Martin, I don't know if you have heard any of the conversations we have been having with Rose?

Considering that we've been shouting our questions so loudly, the rest of the street can hear us, this seems like a pathetic question.

A. It's *Doctor* Jack here,

M. Alfred Jack?

A. *Doctor* Jack.

*It seems he has an ego, this **Doctor** Jack. Maybe I should get him to refer to me as **Inspector** Martin*

M. OK then *Doctor* Jack, how are you?

A. Why are you here, what's happened?

Well Doctor Jack, being an intelligent Doctor, you might have come to realise that you're a hostage and we're trying to release you.

M. The reason we are here is to help you and solve the situation you are in, in there.

A. Well I have Rose in here and we have been chatting and I think I can sort this out if you go and leave us alone.

Oh, is that so, Doctor Jack? Why don't you walk out of there yourself then, if you think you're so bloody clever?

M. What have you been talking about?

A. Her son. She doesn't think you lot have been listening to her, or trying to understand her, so she's not talking to you anymore. She has asked me to talk to you instead. Leave me for twenty minutes, I can solve this, so go away and leave us alone for a while. That would be great.

M. What do you understand to have happened to her son, Phillip?

A. Well, he killed himself.

R. He did not kill himself! It's your fault.

Rose is shouting now. Great work, Dr Perfect, now you have wound up Revengeful Rose

M. Rose? Talk to me, Martin.

R. He did not kill himself! It's down to this Doctor here, this surgery.

M. What actually happened then?

R. He hung himself.

Correct me if I am wrong, but the action of hanging oneself does usually lead to being killed. Still, if I've learnt one thing from the police it's to avoid patronising a crazed arsonist.

R. (*She continues*) He wouldn't have done it if he got the proper treatment. None of this would have happened.

M. Rose, you sound very upset about what happened to Phillip. It's very clear that this was a big effect for you in your life.

No shit Sherlock.

R. (*Crying*) I have taken this to my MP, the solicitor and Coroners Court and it didn't help, he didn't kill himself. If he had had the correct medical care, then none of this would have happened.

M. Do you want to talk to someone else about this?

Other than me perhaps? Because you are crying now, and I feel uncomfortable.

R. Rachel, I have asked already for her to come here, she's my social worker. Is she here yet?

M. We will try and get her here, we have talked to her. If we bring her here will you talk with her?

R. I asked you ages ago if I could speak with Rachel. If she comes here, she will understand. I just want justice, I want to get it recognised it wasn't Phillip's fault.

M. Tell me what happened, help me to understand, talk to me.

R. The doctors didn't help him. Dr Harmsworth.

M. How long ago?

R. 5 years ago.

M. That must have been absolutely awful for you. I can't begin to understand. That must have been so awful for you.

Pretty good, Martin. Emotional labelling and a concerned voice. Rose telling me the facts as she sees them. Much better than my first effort with the store room intercom and the man with the car key fetish.

R. I just want to put the record straight, I can't bring him back.

M. And we can all work on that, together.

R. But no one has listened; I have taken it everywhere I can think of.

M. I am listening; we are listening, out here, that's a start, we are listening. I am very concerned about what has been going on today.

R. Where is Doctor Harmsworth? Because it's really him, he was Phillip's doctor, he can sort it out finally and once he is here we can put it to rest

Is it me, or does her notion of 'putting it to rest' sound a lot like putting Dr Harmsworth to rest? In a blaze of flames, perhaps? It might be time to change the subject.

M. Look, we are trying to get Rachel. If she came here would you come out to talk to her, talk to us, talk to her?

Stop saying talk. Too much talking.

R. Doctor Harmsworth is where it started, so it can end with him.

In a blaze of flaaaaames....

M. I know it's clear you have a great desire to talk to him *(set him on fire)* but he is unavailable.

R. But I can finish it with him.

M. How do you mean finish?

R. Well he was the one treating him when Phillip died.

You didn't answer my question.

M. Right, what do you mean finish?

R. So I can get it straight, it wasn't Phillip's fault, I tried everything else.

M. Rose, we have tried to get Rachel here. We have brought you coffee. We have contacted Doctor Harmsworth. Can you just let Alfred out?

Time for some reciprocity.

R. He doesn't want to come out.

No. Of course he doesn't. He would much rather be in there with you, covered in two litres of unleaded petrol

M. Let him out Rose. You have a gun. You have poured petrol over the place it's not a nice situation for him. (*Bit of an understatement, there*). I am concerned for you and his safety.

R. (*Shouting now*) He has free will and he is choosing to stay in here with me, all right!

Liar, liar, pants on fire. In fact, his pants might actually be on fire soon.

M. I don't know that for sure.

R. He told you to go away and that he was fine, not five minutes ago.

M. I know, but I would rather talk in a nicer environment. I'm here dressed in body armour. The smell of petrol... you have a gun... I'm scared. I don't know about Alfred in there. It would be such a big thing if you let him out, we can get Rachel down here and you can come out to talk with her. Can I leave you alone for a little bit to think about what I have just said?

Yes! I am on a roll.

R. I want to speak with Doctor Harmsworth.

M. I know, but he is unavailable. *(Lucky git)*. Will you at least consider what I have just said before about letting Alfred go?

R. I will consider it.

M. Great, I will leave you for two minutes and come back to you with Rachel's progress.

Saying this was a slight error: we shouldn't set ourselves deadlines and I might not have any new news to give. Never mind. She might not notice. We then go into a team huddle and discuss tactics. We are informed, luckily, that Rachel is on her way. So, we have good news to offer and something else we have done for Rose. After a couple of minutes, I call out to Rose again.

M. Hi Rose, it's Martin again. Are you ready to talk?

R. What do you want to talk about?

M. Have you considered letting Alfred go?

R. Would you like to talk with him?

M. I would, yes, if he is there?

Where else would he bloody be?

R. Doctor Jack?

A. Hello

M. Have you been listening to me and Rose?

A. Of course, I am in the same room as her.

M. What we are trying to do is resolve the situation that you are in down there.

A. What exactly are you doing?

M. Well we have Rachel coming down to the scene, but she is busy at the moment dealing with a serious situation. A life and death situation now.

A. This is a life a death situation here isn't it?

No arguments there.

M. It is indeed.

A. Is it more important than this?

M. Well it's very important this situation, but the other situation- we can't stop that. I don't know what she's dealing with.

A. So what else are you doing?

M. We are trying to contact Doctor Harmsworth, but he is unavailable.

A. I know that, he is on holiday, that's why I am here.

M. Oh he is on holiday, well thank you for telling me that. Now Doctor Jack, how is your heart? I understand that you have angina, do you need any medication?

A. I think I have enough in here thank you, I am fine.

M. I am very concerned about you.

A. What are you doing for Rose, what can you do for her?

M. Well we can talk to her.

A. You have been doing that for hours and have got nowhere.

M. Maybe she can talk again with her MP.

Clutching at straws now, Martin?

A. Is he out there?

Of course. He's standing beside me, patiently eating a cheese and tomato sandwich.

M. Well no, but the only way we can solve this situation is to sit down and talk about your situation. Not like this Rose, it doesn't have to end like this. This situation, the situation can end safely, not like this.

Stop saying situation, Martin

R. If it wasn't for Doctor Harmsworth I wouldn't be in this *situation*.

Now she's at it.

M. But Doctor Jack has done nothing wrong.

R. But he works at the same surgery.

M. I know. But you can't blame everyone that works there at the surgery. You can't blame the surgery. The surgery has other innocent people working there. The only one at the surgery you have an issue with is Doctor Harmsworth, who works at the surgery.

Say surgery one more time Martin, I double dare you.

M. In fact even Rachel, your friend, she is attached to that surgery.

R. All I want is justice for Phillip *(crying again now)*

M. I know, and I can't bear to think what you are going through, you sound so sad.

You really do.

R. No one listens *(crying more now and yelling)*

M. We are listening. I am listening.

R. Talking solves nothing *(crying, yelling and sniffing now)*

There is now so much crying and high-pitched blurb going on, I can't make out what she's saying. I catch the odd word and phrase, 'Phillip', Rachel', 'no one cares', 'Harmsworth's fault.' Things are taking a turn for the worse. I need to think of an epic killer line that will calm her down

M. We can only do, what we can do.

Great statement, Martin. What the hell does that even mean?

R. *(Still yelling and crying)* He hung himself and I found him, he was up the stairs and they said he killed himself and he didn't.

Well technically he did.

R. *(She continues)* He wouldn't do that to his mother, not to me.

Oh, but he did!

M. You actually found him. I mean. God. Awful.

R. All I want is somebody to say it was not his fault. That's all I wanted.

M. And that's all you wanted.

Now we're just going to start mirroring everything that the person in crisis is saying.

R. That's all I wanted.

M. All you wanted.

R. Yes all I wanted.

M. All you wanted.

Enough, Martin.

M. All you needed.

A change of word, wow, I really can't stop myself.

R. I just needed to get him the proper treatment, they are all useless.

M. You just wanted proper treatment.

R. He would never have done that.

M. He never would have done that, he didn't get the treatment he deserved. It was all you wanted.

Now I'm summarising the mirroring, pretty good for a novice.

M. What shall we do, Rachel? What are we to do about this?

Rachel? That's the name of her social worker. Now I am getting my names mixed up. Luckily, this woman is so off her nut she hasn't noticed.

R. I don't know.

M. We have to sort this out, Rachel. There must be other things we can do.

Stop calling Rose, 'Rachel.' Her name is Revengeful Rose.

M. I am very...

(I am stopped mid-sentence by the instructor)

And then it's time to change roles, which if I am honest, I was rather frustrated about. I thought I was doing well. I managed to get emotional labelling, mirroring, summarising and reciprocity into the conversation. There were some good active listening skills displayed there. In fact, I did receive some good feedback from this exercise. Far better feedback than the last exercise I went through. Another colleague then took over from me and did a good job in talking to Rose, or Rachel, or whoever she was. But if you think these scenarios are demanding, boy 'you ain't seen nothin' yet.'

It would take many a year before I could classify myself as a good Negotiator, worthy of assessing others. I quickly found out that it's always good to give a reason for why you want somebody to do something for you: the power of the word *because*. Often it doesn't matter what the reason is, provided there is one. So, when I shouted at this man to come out, I should have said why I wanted him to do so.

If I thought I had trouble thinking of the right words to use in these scenarios, how much harder must it have been for the Japanese student amongst us on the course. He was a lovely gentleman who spoke very little English and yet there he was on a UK Negotiators course! It's hard enough for us Brits to understand the complexities of active listening, but for someone who speaks English as a second language, that bears no resemblance to their own, it becomes downright impossible. Tukka was small in stature, and very calm in a crisis; (Due to the language barrier, I was never sure if he always completely understood if he was actually *in* a crisis during the course)

He was a lovely bloke and his tenacity gave me a bit of hope. If a guy from Japan could get by on this course then bloody hell, so would I.

So, what had I learned during my training?

The course content refers to 'active listening skills' with a view to build rapport, gain trust and influence the person to change their behaviour. Your voice may be your strongest tool and a calm demeanour, and the tone of your voice, is much better than winning an argument. Experience has shown us that kidnappers often like to be in control, so if you were to consistently win an argument against them, then you would be immediately punished, through silence, aggressive threats or the bad guys simply hanging up on you.

There are a number of common mistakes that people make when negotiating, such as trying to get to the end too quickly, interrupting the conversation, telling the suspect too much, or sounding judgemental.

Have you ever tried to explain to a child why she or he can't have that sweet at that time and when they really want it? All you get are tantrums and the repetitive 'I want, I want,' command as they stand there, hands on hips, in an attempt to make themselves look bigger. Yet all you're doing is standing there, trying to explain that dinner time is coming up and you don't want them to ruin their appetite. It's the same with adults and people in a crisis. When someone is angry, or displaying any form of intense emotion, you can't problem solve to any degree because they are simply not listening. You must wait until all the emotion has dissipated and then – only then - can you begin to problem solve. Your words are useless up until this point.

There are also blocks to listening, in that we all love the sound of our own voice. Picture yourself at a dinner party. Someone is recalling some wonderful anecdote about when they went travelling around Thailand to 'find themselves.' But you can't wait to tell them your story of your latest visit to Marks and Spencer's. You find yourself rehearsing your story in your head as they speak, waiting for a gap in the conversation for you to interject. So, you hurry the other person's conversation along and jump to conclusions, finishing their sentences for them, in the rush to get your own thought out. We love the sound of our own voice and nothing seems to upset a kidnapper more than being interrupted. They like to feel in control and they like having their egos massaged. They want and demand respect, so to interrupt is not a good idea. As with my dinner party example, we often give the impression that we are listening, but we are actually deploying deceptive verbal and non-verbal behaviour to hurry the conversation along, so we can say something far more interesting than what the other person is saying - something about y*ou*.

When talking to kidnappers, or people in a crisis, there are certain mistakes that we try and avoid. Too much self-disclosure is a bad thing. It's good to build rapport and attempt to get the other person to like you, because you are always more likely to be able to convince someone who shows some liking towards you. But there is a danger in disclosing too much information. A Negotiator may disclose that he has a family and children for example, in order to empathise with the person they are negotiating with. How far you go with this is a judgement call: you wouldn't want to tell a kidnapper where you live or where your children go to school, if there was a chance they could target you afterwards. It's always a good idea for a Negotiator to know their own open-source profile – Google, Facebook, LinkedIn and any other social media sites. With today's multimedia instant access, it is easy for the person with whom you are conversing to look you up online and use the information to use for their own purposes.

We also shouldn't display a judgemental attitude. It's never a good idea to judge someone who is in a crisis. The act of empathising means being able to leave your own values and judgements at the door. When you judge someone, your dialogue gives it away and you begin to use statements such as 'You should', 'You must,' 'You shouldn't.' A kidnapper might respond to that sort of dialogue with statements like 'Should I now?' and 'Why is that?' or, more likely, 'Don't tell me what to do.' It's better to use softer statements such as 'May I suggest another way to look at this?' or, 'You may be right, but have you thought about ...?'

Over the years, I learned to avoid all of these traps and focus instead on the most important attributes –which in my opinion – would help me as a Negotiator. When we talk to a person in a crisis, we like to develop a *transference*, a positive emotional attitude between the kidnapper/person in crisis and the Negotiator.

Initial attitude is important and it must be a positive one. I work hard at being a person who cares about a successful outcome. I need to portray an objective and non-judgemental attitude and act with Integrity. I show warmth and empathy. As mentioned, I must demonstrate that I respect the individual I'm dealing with and convey a collective spirit, using statement like, '*We* can sort this,' or 'I am sure *we* can find a solution together.'

When most people start off as a 'newbie' Negotiator, they talk like a robot, using no intonation. To the kidnapper, this sounds as if we are reading out of a rule book. It's important not to be monotone, but when we are stressed that's what happens. Look back to the example I transcribed for you from the VCR tape. Note the excessive use of police jargon. To ensure that we do use intonation and sound like a real human being, we go overboard with it in our scenario training. To the stressed person speaking it might sound over the top, but when you play it back to them, what comes out of their mouth just sounds normal. The person in crisis might have a knife to someone's throat, yet we remain polite and never underestimate the worth of saying 'Please' and 'Thank you.' If the person in a crisis sees no way out then we must be helpful to their cause, with phrases such as 'Be optimistic, there's always a solution.' No matter what happens, we appeal to reason.

Active listening requires practice and effort. It is for those moments when something more is at stake. Talking to a kidnapper, a person in a crisis or a hostage is obviously one of those moments. Ordering a pizza isn't, unless extra pepperoni is really important to you. Remember that when it comes to negotiating, both parties have something valuable to say and it's important for us to listen to the entire story before we respond. It helps to give us a full picture and provides clues about the route to a safe outcome. Listening to their justification for their actions will enable us to understand their values and beliefs. We keep the conversation centred on their agenda and do not ask too many questions. It's important to listen to their fears. When in such a scenario, it can often be about saving face. Climbing a crane, threatening to jump off and then changing your mind may require some face-saving strategies. Listening builds trust, which is the key to effective communication. The more a person talks, the more they will disclose.

I progressed from a newbie Negotiator to become an on-call Metropolitan Police Hostage and Crisis Coordinator. It took many years. After I'd graduated from the two-week course, I was not for some time, even permitted to be a 'number one', i.e. the person talking to the person in a crisis. Invariably I was initially posted as a loggist, or as a number two (coach) sitting on the shoulder of the person engaged in dialogue. To me, this made perfect sense as I observed and learned from someone more experienced, to watch how it should be done. After a few incidents, I was eventually promoted up to 'number one', and some years later, after an intensive FBI course, I became a Coordinator and graduated to the international circuit.

The FBI course was held in Quantico, Washington. This was a pleasure and privilege, as it's a difficult course to be selected for and not everyone has that privilege.

On the flight over to Washington I first met Stephen, who I was later to work with on several kidnap cases in Iraq. He was a quiet and unassuming man from a county police force that wasn't a patch on the Met (sorry, biased again). He too had been selected to attend this course and we were to travel together.

We sat on the plane, enjoying our free beers and nuts, in mutual agreement about how much we were looking forward to it. Whilst we didn't come close to having the rigorous skills of the FBI, we knew that American women had a bit of a thing for the English accent and that no matter how our training played out, we were in for a fun time. I remember that it was midway through this discussion that Stephen, tears forming in his eyes, told me he was going through a pretty messy divorce. His wife had been having an affair with his best friend. I spent the remainder of the flight pacifying Stephen and patting him on the back as he sobbed into his bag of peanuts. Negotiating your way through the last ten years of someone else's marriage is never the best way to start a high-profile training course and I was an exhausted mess by the time we touched down. Thankfully Stephen didn't kill himself, although he tried. He ate the Beef Wellington that was being served in Economy and no amount of negotiating could convince him to do otherwise.

We eventually arrived at the hotel that was selected for us by the FBI training team. The place was already packed out with special agents and officers, unbeknownst to the families and tourists also residing there. Imagine if they'd known that the gentlemen sitting opposite them at breakfast, eating their bacon butties and slurping tea were actually trained agents, masters at cyber and domestic crime, weapon handling and counter-intelligence.

The course itself was pretty uneventful and involved two weeks of lectures and practical exercises in a place called Hogan's Alley. I still remember my first assessed exercise. I was negotiating with an armed suspect who was behind the counter in a convenience store with a revolver aimed at someone's head. I remember being told off by the squad leader for standing outside the shop and shouting at the man inside. According to him, I should have entered the shop, walked up to the gun wielding maniac and spoken to him one on one in a brotherly sort of fashion.

I thought this was ludicrous not least because I had no gun, or ballistic body armour. However, being a guest on the course, I'd decided to be humble and keep my mouth shut. Also, they work within an organisation where everyone is armed. Whereas for us from the UK we don't have the mindset to challenge people with firearms, unless we also have one.

The rest of the course was excellent, and it soon became clear to me where our UK officers got most of their material. 'Active listening' was pioneered by the FBI and some days were spent doing only that as our training. Annoyingly my British accent always got in the way of these exercises (I'd forgotten how much terminology and meaning significantly shifts when you venture overseas). In one training scenario I remember trying to talk a distressed individual down from a bridge. Before I even knew what I was saying, out came 'why don't you come down and we'll make you some tea?' That got a tremendous response from the individual, who shouted down at me, 'Tea?' 'Where you from you posh dick?' 'Why don't you come up here for a cup of quaffy, mother fucker?' A bit harsh I thought.

More than anything I'd wanted to leave the course with an FBI T-shirt, only to be told on day four that they weren't available to us upon completing graduation. I did manage to leave with eight FBI clipboards however, as well as a few pens, and a lanyard, which I had traded for Metropolitan Police lapel badges. To this day, I still go to work with my FBI clipboard in the hope that someone will notice and ask me how I manage to own one. It's been thirteen years and still no one has commented. I will have to find other ways to feed my ego.

After this course it was the Coordinator's role that was the one that I coveted. This is the person who will ultimately be in charge of all the Negotiators that are on call at any given time for the whole of London. They are generally of a higher rank, so as to give the role some clout when making strategic decisions during an often fast moving and adrenaline-rushed crisis. The job of a coordinator is to formulate the negotiation strategy and advise the incident commander as to the progress of the negotiation. They must also inform this commander of any demands and deadlines and ask for permission regarding deliveries of food and supplies. They are also responsible for the on-site negotiator's health and safety. This job was the pinnacle of the UK negotiating world, after which it would be time to graduate to become a team leader on the international circuit.

I was fortunate enough to reach the dizzy heights of team leader on the international circuit and to represent the United Kingdom's Foreign and Commonwealth Office on many an overseas kidnap. I carried on with this role right up to when I retired after thirty years of policing. But you can't keep a good man down, so they say, and I sought out a job with a private risk consultancy, where I can use these skills to good effect but within a different environment and context.

This led to another role where I taught companies how to manage kidnaps, and at times use my negotiating skills to assist families and company's crisis management teams, managing international kidnaps and ultimately returning hostages to their loved ones.

So now let's tell some stories that give you a flavour for this bizarre world.

A cranes eye view

To one of my earlier encounters. This incident took place on a very tall crane situated near Victoria Railway Station in London. The crane was part of a large-scale construction project; a building site that was attempting to transform itself into one of those hideously shiny and overpriced shopping arcades.

I was called at five o'clock that afternoon and told to be on standby for an 'emerging incident' in London. It was always commonplace to have negotiators on standby if a crisis looked like it would take longer than five hours. Sure enough, at 5 a.m. I received a call from the coordinator asking me to attend the scene.

It was a crisp and cold December morning, hardly the sort of weather you wanted to be standing in for hours on end without so much as a hot tea or bacon sandwich to keep you toasty. I duly arrived and as I stood in Victoria Street, the negotiator I was to relieve approached me all out of breath and he looked absolutely freezing. He briefed me on the situation so far. A middle-aged Indian man had tied a rope around his neck and was threatening to jump off the top of the crane nearby and kill himself by hanging. This was apparently to avoid being deported from the UK. Negotiations had taken place throughout the night and had achieved nothing.

Quite often the second negotiator that gets called to the scene (this time me) will be the one to solve the incident. Firstly, because calling a second negotiator to the scene demonstrates to the person having the crisis just how long the situation could go on for unless they conclude the incident. After all, there's never any shortage of negotiators on hand and the coordinator can re-call them in shifts to their hearts content. In many a scenario I have left the scene only to return twelve hours later to the same victim, still out on a ledge, still and still threatening to jump.

The other reason for the second negotiator's success is that they come in at a vital turning point in the negotiating process. By the time they arrive the emotional issues of the victim have been thoroughly ploughed through and all their anger, frustration and anxiety has been reduced. This immediately creates an environment in which problem solving and logical thinking can be achieved, which makes it a lot easier to convince said person to get down/come out/stop being difficult.

'He still has the rope around his neck,' the negotiator informs me. 'I think this one might actually jump.' He goes on to explain that the man in question, Syed, is really cold and asking for a blanket. He also wants his case for deportation re-examined as he believes he'll be persecuted if he's forced to return to India.

The operational plan is to wait until his solicitor's office opens later in the morning to explore this as a possibility and at the very least offer him an extended residency until his case can be examined. My immediate plan however is to keep Syed from jumping off the crane and I hope that in knowing this, he'll feel some hope for his situation.

To make him aware of my plan however, I need to go all the way up the crane and speak to him. I don't know if you've ever given any thought to how long it takes to climb up a crane (I certainly hadn't until that moment) but twenty minutes after launching off I was still climbing. By the time I got to the top I could barely feel my forearms from grabbing onto the metal ladder that snakes up the middle.

Every negotiator receives training from the Metropolitan Police Rope Team (before you ask, yes, they are a real team, though somewhat stupidly coined). The instructors attached to this team teach us the basic skills of climbing. Skills like how to anchor on to a building roof by using a range of bonding items. This ensures that no deranged individual can take you along with them if they do decide to run at you and jump. Part of the equipment we're supplied with look like huge metal crab claws, which you clamp onto ladder rungs and then attach through a belt harness to ensure that you don't fall. It's all super sexy 007 type stuff.

Our involvement in this scenario was one of typical suicide intervention and the most important thing to do in a situation such as this is to look for *hooks* in the person's conversation to try to get them to rethink their behaviour. A suicidal person can feel any one of the following emotions: hopelessness, helplessness, guilt, loneliness, separation, abandonment, or any combination. We try to look out for indirect clues that might indicate what they're feeling. Statements like 'You won't have to ring me much more', 'I can't go on', 'I will resolve the problem my way' and even 'everyone is better off without me' are all suggesting that the person's not in a good way.

It's important that we try to de-fuse these intense emotions and return the person to normal functioning behaviour. We do our best to be non-judgemental and non-analytical. We avoid lecturing them and we offer support where we can. It's also important to try to reduce the immediate danger of the situation they're in, which means trying to rid the person of items that may cause them harm, be it knives, drugs, guns or in this case a rope around their neck. If we're not sure whether they're suicidal we can ask them. At least we will then be more aware what we are dealing with.

We will ask them to talk about their thoughts, speaking slowly and using simple words. It's important that we focus on the cause of their suicidal feelings. We avoid using phrases like 'I understand what you are going through' because the first thing that will get thrown back in our faces is 'how can *you* possibly understand what *I'm* going through?' We can never *fully* understand, but we can do our best to offer empathy and a way out.

To ensure that their emotions are reduced we also try to get them to direct their anger at us. This acts as an outlet and usually leaves them feeling calmer. Finally, we will try to explore what is meaningful to the person and get them to cling on to that to develop a realistic plan of action.

So, there I was at the top of the girder, arms throbbing, feeling slightly dizzy and also, if I'm honest, feeling completely out of breath.

The dialogue below shows the exchange between Syed and me. There were only two of us up there, but I've included a brief cast list for clarity nonetheless.

M. Martin

S. Syed

M. So that was tiring.

I look around expecting a reply before realising, as I frantically scan the area, that I can't see anyone. Did he jump just before I got to the top? *How bloody inconsiderate*, I think to myself, *twenty minutes of climbing for nothing*. Then I look left and down and see, on the horizontal section of the crane, a very cold looking Indian man who looks scared, desperate and indeed hopeless. He had been up there all night after all and now here he was, standing defiantly with a makeshift noose around his neck, which was tied to the crane girders by his feet. My colleague who had been speaking to him previously the night before had informed me that he had been close to jumping on a number of occasions. I realised then that unlike the attention seekers I was usually faced with in such suicide interventions, this guy was a kind and good person, who actually deserved my help. And I decided that I would do my best for him, that I would ensure that he got down safely and that he got the assistance he required. I also noticed at this point that I was swaying in the wind. I'm not the biggest fan of heights so decided that rather than crawling out onto the horizontal section of the crane to join Syed, I'd remain near the driver's cabin at the top of the stairs. I thought this would also satisfy Syed as he would be aware that I couldn't physically interfere with his plans to top himself. I took my position crouched on my knees at the beginning of the girder, at the top of the steps by the driver's cab and began to shout.

M. So I hear *(pant, pant)* you are very concerned about your deportation *(pant, pant)*. Is that correct?

Syed shouts back.

S. I am not going back. I told your friend. Come closer and I will jump!

M. I know that. That's why we are going to contact a solicitor to look into your case and try and delay this for you. Their office opens at 9 a.m. in a couple of hours. That's good news, yes?

S. I am not going or leaving this country?

'Oi, oi!'

I hear some shouting from below. As I look down, standing between the girders, are five reflective jackets all huddled together on a flat roof; builders about to begin their days' work on the site. Terrific, I think. The last thing you need in a situation like this is an audience. Onlookers do nothing but disrupt rapport and delay our progress. When we negotiate with people who are high up over London it can be fairly difficult to isolate the person from the public gaze, but we always do our best to make sure the incident can't be seen. If they're at ground level, we often use police cordons to avoid public interruptions and will even take to closing off streets or diverting cars and buses if we have to. The one thing you can't do however is start evacuating buildings which means that many people will inevitably manage to see what's going on. They'll even open their doors to media crew so that they can get a look in and extend the spectacle.

The crane we were standing on was overlooking one of the busiest streets in central London. If Syed were to jump, he would land beside a number of building skips inside the site. Luckily this meant that no passing pedestrians would be injured, though they might get some surprise at seeing a potential deportee soaring through the air towards them.

'You gonna jump or what?' I hear the builders sneer from the girder below. I shake my head. Those pricks think they're so humorous, but if Syed actually jumped as a result of their words, then odds are they'd regret it for the rest of their lives.

'Guys,' I shout down. 'That's really not very helpful. I am a police officer and I'm trying to save this man's life.'

I hear sniggers as they nudge each other, slurp their tea and eat their bacon rolls. I need to remain calm in view of Syed although what I'd really like to do is shout down to the builders and tell them all to fuck off or they will all be nicked, and that they should go find their fun elsewhere. Instead, being the professional that I am, I call my coordinator and ask him to arrange for their removal.

Oh yes. I almost forgot social media. Nowadays, everyone has a camera thanks to smartphones. In the negotiating world this means that we get an awful lot of observers beaming images from their phones straight on to networking sites, which are then picked up by news crews and the press. Recently one guy took a selfie with a hijacker whilst still on the plane! Such imagery can be damaging for us and for the person in a crisis, as they can access their phone and see what is being reported about them. This can then have a negative impact on our negotiations. To counteract this we try and convince the person that most of what is being reported is false and that they should ignore it. Some of the people we deal with however actually like the attention and play up to it. Syed on the other hand clearly wanted to be left alone.

M. Don't listen to them. We will get them removed.

S. Idiots.

M. Of course they are. Just focus on me.

S. I'm freezing.

M. I'm not surprised. I am exhausted after climbing those steps and I don't particularly like heights. But I wanted to come here today to help you and I will stay with you to try and sort this out.

It's a good idea when negotiating to try to remind the person of what you've done for them as it makes things personal. We call this 'positive police actions' and it's to encourage some act of reciprocity. We all feel obliged to return favours. If I buy you a drink, you'll feel obliged to buy me one (unless you're a cheap skate and one of those types that always hangs around at the back of the group, goes to the bar last and drinks really slowly). When a kidnapper turns around and says, 'What have you done for me copper?' you can reply and tell them exactly what you have done. At times we haven't actually done a lot, but many small things presented together sound more impressive. For example, not arresting them, not lying to them, not ignoring their requests, treating them seriously, always answering the phone when they have rung, promising to bring a solicitor to the scene and not entering the premises to arrest them. After presenting such actions we may then ask for something in return. We don't always get such a commitment, but they may be under more pressure to do offer something.

M. I want to help you, Syed.

S. Why? You don't know me.

M. I would like to know you. You seem to care for your family and not wanting to leave them to fend for themselves.

Boy, this crane sways a lot in the wind.

M. Windy up here isn't it? And you have been here all night?

S. Yup and they won't give me a blanket.

That's because we don't want you to get too comfortable when you're way up high and threatening to jump. Because if you're comfy, you'll be up here even longer. And then so will I. if I am honest I really don't want to be up here for 12 hours.

We often use luxuries as a temptation for the person to come down and surrender. I remember teasing one suicidal chap, Tim, with the power of hunger. He was standing on a bridge over a railway line and had kept complaining about wanting a chicken kebab. (People in a crisis can be very specific about their food requests). We made him talk about how much he wanted this kebab. What salad he wanted with it, what type of bread, what sauce, until he had a complete visual of it and was practically salivating before our eyes. Then my colleague trotted off and before long came back with three kebabs. We sat down to eat them, making sure to place the third kebab on a wall beside us in plain sight of the man on the bridge. All the better to implement our tease tactic. As we sat there munching away, dropping lettuce from the edges and making extremely loud 'yummy' noises, I could see Tim the jumper looking over desperately hungrily.

T. Give it here, then.

M. Pardon?

T. The fucking kebab.

Now to tease

M. If you want the kebab mate, it's here for you. And hot it is too, just as you wanted. But you have to come down for it. If you come down, I promise you can have it.

T. Wankers.

M. Well like I say, the longer you are up there the colder it will become.

Tease more.

M. Do you want it hot?

And more.

T. Of course!

M. Are you really hungry?

T. You fucking know I am!

M. Well?

Two minutes later, after a lot of loud munching and wiping sauce from our chins, we were joined by our sad looking jumper, fresh off the bridge and come to eat his kebab.

Anyway, back to the crane.

M. I'm afraid we have no blanket. But if you come down you can wrap up warm and have some breakfast.

S. Like I said to your other negotiator, I will come down when I can stay in the country.

Another reason most people decide to come down is because they are desperate for the toilet. At times I like to think it's down to my expert skills, rather than a piss requirement, but I will always claim it was my skill nevertheless. Syed had been up there for over seven hours and must at the very least needed a toilet break. I'm about to ask him if he needs to go when I suddenly hear something that sounds a lot like snoring. I look around. Syed and I are both awake, so I have no idea where this noise is coming from. I look towards the crane operators' cabin and peer inside. Sure enough towards the glass sided control box is a sleeping lump of bearded, fat, farting, snoring crane operator.

I decide to wake him because he is asleep, and I am not, which is really irritating me.

'Morning!' I shout at him. He shuffles, stretches, yawns, scratches his arse and slowly sits up.

'Oh hello mate, you still talking to him then?'

Oh no, I consider replying. I just popped up here for a tourist view of London and to deliver some breakfast for you.

'I was wondering,' I begin, ignoring his question, 'if you need to take a piss up here, what do you do?'

I see him think for a moment then reach into a corner and pick up a plastic bag, from inside which he produces an orange juice container.

'I do it in here, mate.'

Hmm, better than doing it on people below I suppose.

He points to where Syed is standing. 'I think you'd better look, mate' he says. I turn and notice that Syed is tightening the noose around his neck. I hear the workers down below shouting 'Jump, you tosser!'

What is it with these people?

I shout out, 'Alright, Syed, what are you doing?'

Although it looks bloody obvious

S. Nothing, just making sure.

M. Of what exactly?

S. That it will do the job.

M. It looks pretty tight to me, although it would be easier to chat if you took it off. I mean, I am certainly not walking out there and you would have time to put it back on, even if I did. Although like I say, I doubt I would come to you as it looks pretty scary.

It's always good to be honest and show some weakness in these scenarios. It makes the other person feel more in control or at least less reticent to confess to the same feelings, which in turn gives them an opportunity to save face and surrender.

I look down to see the builders being marched away by uniformed police. The coordinator must have contacted the local police commander and got him to remove the distraction. I look back to Syed and see him holding his noose and staring out over the edge to the busy Victoria Street below.

M. Syed!

S. Yup?

M. You have highlighted your cause. We are ensuring that you can speak to a solicitor this morning. You have shown how desperate you are. Now's the time to come with me so we can re-examine your case.

What else do you want me to do? Tell me and I will do it so that I can get down off this crane that's swaying like crazy.

S. I need more of a guarantee

Fine, I hereby guarantee Syed that he can remain in the country forever.

M. I'm worried that you are now so cold you may slip. Will you allow me to at least get a harness to you, so that you can secure it to the crane in case you fall unintentionally?

S. Fall unintentionally? I want to jump deliberately!

Ah, good point.

M. I know, but this will keep you safe whilst you choose to remain on the crane. What do you say?

Ah ha, got him!

S. Fine.

It's always a good sign when a person contemplating suicide wants to keep themselves safe. I was getting very cold by this point and the excess heat I'd built up from climbing the crane was exiting from the top of my head like steam.

S. Have you got a blanket?

M. No, sorry.

S. It's freezing.

M. Well why don't you come down with me and have a nice cup of tea and put on some warmer clothes?

S. Why can't you bring me one? Your colleague last night was much nicer to me.

Yes, maybe that would explain why you're still up here after seven hours of negotiating mate.

There comes a time in the negotiating process where we have to become more assertive. To do that we start using more 'I' statements to show the individual how we feel about the actions and words they're using. For example, *'When you keep shouting that you want one million dollars and then don't listen to my reply, I feel frustrated.'*

Here is a rough guide on how to be assertive in negotiations. The first statements under headings may be used during a financial kidnapping, whilst the second statements may be used during a suicide intervention.

First, describe how you view the situation.

1. *'You refuse every offer we have made.'*

2. *'You keep walking close to the edge.'*

Let the other person know how the situation makes you feel.

1. *'I feel frustrated because that's all the money we have.'*

2. *'I feel anxious in case you slip and fall off.'*

State the effects of the other person's behavior upon yourself or others.

1. *'Your constant refusal to acknowledge this offer means that we don't move forward to an agreement.'*

2. *'This prevents us from talking about the issues at hand because I am spending all my time asking you to take care and be safe.'*

Wait for a response, whilst reflecting your understanding of both the content and feelings of their response.

1. *'Am I right in thinking that you need the amount to be increased and that your boss is unhappy with the offer? I am sorry to hear that he is disappointed, that was not my intention.'*

2. *'So it seems from what you are saying that you are doing this to make me realise that you are serious about jumping.'*

Indicate what you would like the outcome to be. Indicate what the consequence will be for not following your suggested path.

1. *'I would like you to accept this offer so that we can deliver it to you, otherwise we can't move forward.'*

2. *'May I suggest that you walk towards me away from the edge, so we can talk about you coming down safely?'*

I ask for a harness to be brought up to me by the fire brigade who I noticed at the scene on my arrival. They were parked up off the side of the road, waiting like coiled springs ready for action. I tell Syed of my plans.

M. I am going to get the fire brigade to bring a harness up to you.

S. Whatever.

I decide to sit in silence as we wait for the harness to arrive. I want to allow Syed time to reflect on his thoughts.

After thirty minutes a rugged fireman arrives and hands me a canvass harness. Annoyingly he doesn't seem at all out of breath from the journey he's taken. But I guess he's used to ladders? I look out to Syed again. He's now sitting down and staring at the pavement below, deep in thought. I call out to distract him from his probable morose musings.

M. Syed, here's the harness we discussed. Let me throw it to you. Put it on and attach yourself to the crane. It can be unhooked at any time. I will need to come closer to throw it to you. Is that OK?

S. Fine.

M. Thank you.

Gingerly I edge out to the horizontal girder and creep towards him on hands and knees. The girders are bloody freezing and hurting my knees. I really must man up. I really hate heights like this. I get within twenty feet of Syed and chuck the harness, which lands neatly at his feet. With gritted teeth, I start to slowly edge my way backwards along the girder towards the driver's cab.

M. Be careful as you put it on, I shout back.

S. No funny business.

M. No, no funny business. As you can see, I'm crawling back (as quick as I can).

And then it happens. As Syed is trying to keep the noose on whilst attaching the harness, he slips. Luckily for him he has already attached the harness to the girder. I see him regain his balance and catch his breath. The shock has clearly got to him.

S. OK! OK! I'm coming down. I nearly fell!

Nearly fell? Wasn't that what he wanted?

M. OK. But wait there until I get the fire brigade to carry you down in a harness. Your hands are very cold and you might not be able to hold on as you descend. You might slip and fall.

S. Good idea.

Good idea? The man who's kept the whole of a building site closed for ten hours due to his suicide mission now thinks it's a good idea to be lowered back to ground level in a harness in case he falls and hurts himself. The tables turn quickly in this line of work.

We call down to the fire brigade. They arrive twenty minutes later (again not remotely short of breath), put Syed into his harness and slowly, over a period of thirty minutes, help him down to street level.

I remain up in the driver's cab having a chat with the man that has the best view of London and pisses in an orange juice container at will.

I look down and see Syed being handed over to the local uniform police, who drive him off to the local station to make sure his deportation is looked into as promised.

I say goodbye to my crane operator friend and head back down. Going down was much easier for sure and after a cup of tea, I debrief my boss.

'Why did he come down, then?' my boss asks me inquisitively.

'Oh, well you know. My skill in building rapport and deploying my active listening clearly helped to change his mind.'

He looks at me blinking and repeats the question. 'Why did he *really* come down, Martin?'

It's clear my bullshit isn't working, so I decide to be honest. 'Honestly? He slipped and fell, then panicked so he decided to come down.'

My boss smiles at me. It seems that yet again the presence of a well-trained negotiator has helped draw another dangerous incident to a safe and swift conclusion. Yeah right.

Batman on the Abbey

Now away from suicide interventions and onto demonstrations and protesters.

Fathers 4 Justice, or F4J as it is more pithily coined, was formed in the summer of 2001 by a London-based Creative Director and political activist Matt O'Connor after he was denied access to see his two boys in Britain's Family Courts. This followed a difficult separation from his first wife.

Despite resolving the matter out of court in late 2001 and re-establishing a normal relationship with his children, O'Connor pledged to reform family law for the benefit of his two sons whom he feared would suffer the same experience when they became fathers. On 17th December 2002, F4J staged their first direct action demonstration and two hundred Father Christmas's stormed the lobby of the Lord Chancellor's Department.

O'Connor masterminded the creation of one of the highest profile campaign groups in the world, spawning a host of imitation groups in different countries. His iconic protests have garnered worldwide publicity for a cause shrouded in secrecy by the courts and ignored by the political and religious elite.

From Spiderman on Tower Bridge, to Batman on a ledge at Buckingham Palace and the flour-bombing of the British Prime Minister in the chamber of the House of Commons, the campaign for truth, justice and equality in family law has captured the public imagination, catapulting the issues surrounding it to the top of the political agenda, whilst inspiring thousands of disenfranchised parents and grandparents alike to campaign for equal parenting rights.

The call came in at around 9am, on a lovely warm and sunny Saturday morning. 'Martin, we have a demonstration at Westminster Abbey. Batman has climbed onto the Abbey.'

'Sorry? Can you repeat that?' I replied, unsure of what I'd heard.

The voice on the other end sighed. 'We think it's Fathers for Justice. You know, the people who dress up as super heroes?'

I could briefly recall persuading a Spiderman to come down from Tower Bridge eight months ago. I'd struggled to contain my chuckles at the time. After seeing a middle-aged man's lycra-clad belly, the ability to take them seriously becomes a pretty dim prospect.

So, a weekend ruined by a cartoon character, at least it got me out of mowing the lawn. I pack my notes and head off to the allocated Rendezvous Point, which should take me half an hour.

Sure enough, as I arrived at the scene, again on Victoria Street, I could make out an enormous banner with the words 'Fathers for Justice' emblazoned across a façade of Westminster Abbey. Standing below this banner, on an outside balcony, stood a very triumphant looking Batman who was about fifty feet up from street level. I noticed, no sign of a Robin. I parked my car, wondering if I'd get a glimpse of the Batmobile any time soon, and went off to find the local police Inspector who was in charge of cordoning off the area to prevent Batman from leaving and the public from getting too close to the cape crusader.

I parked my car and approached the Inspector, as I was dressed in civilian clothes, I showed him my police warrant card to identify myself to him. He looked at me with a strained smile and began his briefing. 'He's protesting for cause. He says he's not coming down until he is mentioned in the Abbey service tomorrow by the Dean of Westminster.'

'Fat chance,' I replied. Could he really see that happening? Perhaps he'd also like us to shine a light with the F4J logo into the sky. I was the first negotiator on scene and immediately went over to the bottom of the Abbey and stood underneath the balcony. I shouted up to Batman with my usual introduction.

M. Hello, my name is Martin. I am with the police, and I am here to help.

B. Really?

M. Yes, so what's up?

Do I call him Batman?

B. Listen mate, you know who we are, right?

Yes, I presume you're an F4J campaigner with a lame obsession for Batman.

M. Please tell me.

B. Fathers for Justice. And where's Robin?

He's asking me?

M. Robin?

B. Yeah, Robin. Where is he?

M. Isn't he with you?

B. Look mate stop mucking around, you lot have got him.

OK this is getting surreal.

M. I'm sorry, but I haven't been told that we have anyone.

I glance around to see the uniformed inspector I spoke to earlier.

M. Just hang on a minute, will you? I am going to find out if the local cops know anything.

I head over to the inspector who is yawning wearily and shovelling sweets in his gob.

M. Hello there, would you know anything about the location of Robin?

I. Yup, he's been nicked.

M. I see. Can I ask what for? Batman up there is concerned.

I. Trespassing on this iconic building. He was a bit slow behind the other one, didn't get up the ladder in time, so we grabbed him.

Terrific, now I have to tell Batman that his cape crusader team mate's been nicked. This sort of news really isn't helpful for building rapport. I approach the bottom of the Abbey to speak to

Batman again, who by this point is leaning against the balcony and smoking a cigarette with an air of boredom.

M. Hi. Me again. By the way, what should I call you?

B. Batman, of course!

M. Of course. Well Batman, I have some news regarding your partner in crime. I'm afraid he has been arrested.

I take a few steps back, anticipating a barrage of verbal abuse. But I'm pleasantly surprised.

B. Fair enough. Well, I want to speak to him and make sure he is OK. And I ain't coming down until our demands are met. Got it?

Now part of me has sympathy for F4J. At the time of the launching of their first campaign, I was going through a divorce myself and having a great deal of trouble with my own access rights. I have found that the people in this organisation are not bad, just misunderstood and usually at their wits end, or so it seemed to me. They'd exhausted every avenue, and however attention seeking their ploys might seem, they performed them only out of a love for their children.

M. Let's talk about why you are up there, then.

B. Let's!

Do I detect sarcasm?

M. Right, so tell me. I'm here to listen.

B. OK big guy, then listen to this. Tomorrow there's a sermon in Westminster Abbey and a well-known woman MP (Member of Parliament) is addressing the congregation. I want her to highlight our cause.

Really an MP? Does he really think she's going to speak out on his behalf?

M. What exactly would you like to happen?

B. For her to stand up in front of them and acknowledge our plight to draw some attention to us.

Draw attention to you? You're dressed as Batman and standing on the top of Westminster Abbey. You've stopped the traffic in Parliament Square. You've drawn a large crowd. You've tied up police resources. You are being reported on the news and in traffic warnings. How much more attention could you possibly want mate?

M. I will investigate this for you.

Note my attempt at reciprocity?

M. It sounds like a very difficult thing for us to do though.

Cue managing his expectations.

M. I would like you to come down though.

B. I will when this is done for me.

I decide to paraphrase the situation we're in, for clarity's sake.

M. So your intention is to stay up there until a member of the government addresses the congregation tomorrow?

B. Yup.

Right. So now I have his demands, and a commitment to come down. I'm rather chuffed at the speed with which we came to agree on this. The demands he's made are entirely unachievable at this time and very unlikely to ever come into fruition. I know that this MP has no children of her own and might therefore have no sympathy or understanding towards the F4J plight. To be honest given her love of cats (if certain documentaries are to be believed) she seems like the sort of middle-aged woman to see a lack of access to young children as a blessing, not a curse, so she wouldn't begin to understand what these fathers were complaining about. I consider the situation carefully. If Batman stays where he is throughout today and the rest of tomorrow it will cost the police a great deal of time and resource. It will also inconvenience a lot of people. I'm of half a mind to deploy a tactical team to scale the walls and jump him. My thoughts are interrupted.

B. What about Robin?

Oh, give it a rest mate.

M. I will ensure that Robin is fine for you. I understand that he was arrested because he wasn't quick enough getting up there with you, is that right?

B. No, he was arrested because you lot don't like us.

'You lot' being who exactly, the Metropolitan Police Anti Marvel Comic Squad?

M. Well, whatever the reason, I will ensure he is looked after. Now then, your request about the MP speaking to the congregation is quite a large one. I will have to speak to the Dean of Westminster about it. As I'm sure you can understand, I have no authority over what happens in the Abbey. But I will do my best for you.

B. Best you do, as I ain't coming down until my demand is met, got it?

M. What about a compromise so you can come down now? You have a lot of publicity all ready. Look, there are TV cameras turning up, all of them broadcasting about your demonstration today. Surely this is sufficient-

I am interrupted by his ringing mobile phone. He holds a finger up to his lips to silence me so he can answer it. I hear him speaking to someone in a low, gruff voice.

M. Who are you talking to?

He doesn't reply. It's times like these, when the person you're negotiating with ignores you, that you begin to feel slightly inadequate. I stand silently, twiddling my thumbs, thinking about where Batman purchased his ensemble, or whether he did not in fact purchase it and it's just a rental-

B. Oi!

I find my thoughts interrupted by Batman, who is now standing over the railing and shouting down at me in irritation, his phone call obviously over.

M. Oh, are you done? I didn't want to disturb your call.

B. Shouldn't you be chatting to the Dean?

M. I thought you might consider my recent request for you to come down earlier.

B. I did, and no, I don't want to. So, go and talk to the Dean.

He's getting bossy now. Clearly, he's impatient. No wonder his wife doesn't want him seeing his kids. She probably thinks it's damaging for her children to repeatedly witness their father dressed as a Bat.

M. Are you sure that this MP is attending tomorrow? And what else do you know about this service? It seems like you have carried out some research.

B. I have, yes, and it will gain us more publicity.

M. They won't allow cameras inside.

B. I know, but people will hear about what we have done.

Which will make the government change their legislation laws, allowing father's access to their children whenever they should feel the need, lest the capital be overrun with superheroes. Yes, it is a flawless logic.

M. So have you got supplies up there to keep you going?

B. Don't worry about me mate, I have enough. I'm all set until you give me what I want.

I decide to walk off and give Batman a bit of time to reflect. Admittedly, he has done pretty well for himself. He's scaled a famous London landmark dressed like a bat and publicised his cause to the world without using violence. Whilst he's managed to lose his sidekick in the process, that hasn't affected the hold he has on London.

I head over to the local inspector, who asks me how the negotiations are going. I smile and tell him it's going tremendously well, before telling him the demands that batman has made. The inspector laughs and shakes his head.

I. No chance in hell

M. Thanks. It's worth asking though, right?

I. No.

I sense that today, no one wants to help me out.

M. Well, I would like you to find the Dean, so I can at least put this demand to him.

I. OK, I will find out where he is.

He walks off, talking into his radio, no doubt in an attempt to locate the desired Dean. I decide to get myself a latte from a local cafe. The constant craning and shouting up at Batman has fuelled my desire for caffeine and some energy.

Ten minutes later (tall latte with extra shot in hand), I'm met by a fellow negotiator who asks me how the situation fares. I tell him the demand and that it is unlikely to be met and ask him if he has any insightful ideas. He doesn't. I glance around and watch the tourists gathering. They're mostly Japanese and waving their arms at the sight of Batman on top of the ledge, parading around like a movie star on a film set. It's annoying from our point of view when the person we're negotiating with craves attention and then gets it. It feeds their ego, making them less willing to comply with our requests.

It's a nice weekend in central London, in an area of famous landmarks and buildings, so attempting to get rid of hundreds of camera wielding Japanese tourists is an impossible task. This means we're probably resigned to keeping the area open and allowing Batman the attention he so craves. I head back over to Batman who is now leaning against the Westminster balcony and tucking into a sandwich wrapped in silver foil. He really did come prepared!

M. It's me again. I guess you've noticed all these tourists taking your picture. That's an awful lot of publicity for you. I'm trying to locate the Dean in the meantime.

B. Great. Thanks.

M. So, what happens if he says no? Surely you've considered this possibility?

B. Yeah, but we'll just have to make sure he says yes.

M. But even if *he* does, Ms 'Government Minister' might decline.

B. She might.

M. So, then what?

B. Then you influence them to do as I have asked.

It seems Batman is even more strong willed than I realised. Of course, what he's failed to tell us is, what he'll do if his request is refused, which he knows. He may come down. He may stay up there and keep making demands. We may have to go and get him. I have been informed that a 'rope team' have already been dispatched. Their job will be to climb up there to be close to him, firstly to ensure he is safe, secondly to get me up there with him, which will make my negotiating job a little easier and save my voice a little. One of my jobs is to inform Batman that the rope team will be arriving, will situate themselves close to him and that this will enable me to secure myself nearer so our conversation to be easier. By fully explaining the reasons there will be no surprises and no freaking out the winged super hero up there. His only thoughts maybe that we are going to grab hold of him, but if I am convincing enough he might not protest too much.

M. So, we have a team of officers who are part of our rope team. They need to come up to the balcony and ensure that you are safe. From that location I might come up there also, so I can chat to you properly without having to shout. Is that OK?

B. If you try and come near me, I will jump and it will be your fault.

M. That won't happen. It's really just to make me secure so that I can talk to you. Health and safety and all that.

I turn around to suddenly see the Dean making his way towards us, dressed in his majestic regalia. I am introduced by the inspector and I politely shake his hand, informing him of Batman's request.

D. I have no problem with this. All God's creatures have their plights. I am happy to assist it if it stops this man from doing something reckless. Allow me to see what can be arranged.

Eh? Really?

M. Thank you my lord, eminence, Deanship.

I was never clear on ecclesiastical terminology. I head over, all excited and slightly perplexed, to tell Batman.

M. I have some great news!

B. What?

M. The Dean has agreed to consider your request.

B. Hmm. Well, Okay. Good.

I'm beginning to understand why this guy is in the middle of a divorce. Is he ever impressed with the efforts made in order to satisfy his needs by anyone?

M. Of course, we must remember that the Dean isn't the only one making decisions.

B. Whatever.

Grumpy git. Soon it's time for me to go up there for a cosy chat. The rope team arrive and I secure myself into the rope harness before walking up the inside stairs to the external balcony where Batman is standing. It's pretty high up and I'm grateful for the harness. I see a few Japanese tourists standing below, taking pictures of me and shaking their heads. Perhaps they're disappointed that I'm not in costume. Although I could create one, North Face Fleece Man!

M. (I look in the eyes of the masked one) Hello again. It's quite high up here, isn't it? Your ladder must have been big!

B. Big enough to get me up here. No funny business mind, I want you to keep back.

M. Don't worry I'm not coming any closer than I need to.

Now that I'm up there alongside him, and no longer shouting from street level, his tone begins to change. He starts to become chatty and even asks me a few questions.

B. So you got kids?

M. Yup, two.

B. You divorced?

M. Yup.

B. So you see your kids?

M. I do, yes.

B. Lucky you.

M. You don't see yours?

B. She restricts me to every other weekend, which I consider unfair. The courts always rule in the woman's favour. What's fair in that?

I feel this is the perfect opportunity to empathise and build rapport.

M. Sounds like you feel the courts have let you down

No reply.

M. So tell me what happened.

B. She is a bitch. She says I'm violent and that the kids hate me. All women are mad. She says I don't pay towards their keep. But she was having an affair. All women are mad.

M. It sounds like you feel really misunderstood.

You poor grumpy individual.

B. That's an understatement. Anyway, don't think I don't know what you're doing mate. Trying to chat away to catch me off guard, so you can persuade me to come down before tomorrow. I'm long in the tooth, mate. I have done this before. Chat away. I ain't coming down until my demands are met.

Batman is beginning to annoy me, yet I can't help but feel sympathy for his plight. I think for a minute, briefly considering whether I should join his protest. After all, I don't like my ex and I want to see a lot more of my kids too. Perhaps someone can dig me out a Buzz Light-year outfit for me to wear. Then again, I don't want to sleep on a ledge all night. I have an evening out planned. (Although I would love to shout 'to infinity and beyond' at those tourists below).

We chat on for a few more minutes but the conversation is circular. ('Are you going to come down?' 'No.' 'What can I do to make you come down?' 'Nothing.')

I decide to go back down and swap with the other negotiator. The Dean is standing there when I get down, not to mention about a hundred cameras and members of the press behind him, all beaming down on us waiting to get a statement. The cameras click away. I approach the Dean.

D. So, good news. The MP has agreed to mention Fathers for Justice, highlight their cause and explain what they're doing on the balcony.

M. Fuck me! Whoops, er, blimey, sorry for swearing Dean.

D. Surprised?

M. Absolutely. That's great though. I will let him know.

I climb back up to Batman's balcony, the attempted enthusiasm in my voice spilling out of me like lava.

M. Guess what!

B. Dunno. What?

M. The Dean says yes to your request. Isn't that the best news? Look what you've achieved today! I guess you might as well come down now.

B. Ha! Yeah, right.

M. Look, he's completely trustworthy. You don't think the Dean of Westminster would lie to the police, do you?

B. Well the Church is probably one of the biggest secret organisations in the world. So yes, I do.

M. Okay. So what next?

B. When it's done, I come down.

There I was, destined to remain here on this ledge talking to a Marvel cartoon character. I could see the plans for my night out crumbling before me. I decided that the next time *I* wanted something I was going to climb onto a really tall building and shout various demands at passers-by. 'I want a pay rise!' 'I want more paid leave!' Clearly the best way to get anything in this world is by being a demanding, being an infuriating pain in the arse and bring central London to a standstill.

B. So if you are staying with me until tomorrow, what are we going to talk about? And don't try any funny business like rushing me or anything.

M. I have never lied to you and I won't. You can trust me. All I want to do is get you to come down safely. I would obviously like you to come down now. But I want you to trust me that you will be well looked after, be allowed legal representation and I will ensure that all this happens for you. You have achieved a lot and got your demands. No one is going to rush you, that wouldn't be the safe way to solve this.

B. OK, cheers. I think you make a lot of sense, actually I think I might-

Suddenly I was pushed aside. Capes were twirling. Masks were being ripped off. Screams of 'you traitor!' could be heard alongside the sounds of scratching, punching, pulling and shoving. That's the thing about negotiating. You never know when a rescue attempt or forceful arrest will be made. There I was, trampled on the ground as several macho looking officers put Batman into handcuffs.

Harnesses were strapped to him. Ropes were attached. Slowly (and still struggling) he was walked down the precarious staircase. He was then transported off in a police van to somewhere. To this day I have no clue what charges were brought against him. Probably criminal trespass or some obscure piece of legislation that makes it a crime to climb on religious buildings. Talking of obscure legislation, did you know its still an offence to beat your doormat in the street after 8am? And so is disturbing any inhabitant by knocking at any door without lawful excuse! Interesting eh?

As I was leaving, I kept a keen eye around the site for any sign of a parked Batmobile, before realising, with disappointment, that my caped companion had probably taken a bus to the Abbey.

Burglar Bill and his mum

The previous two incidents have shown that my actual negotiating has not brought the event to conclusion, but instead unforeseen circumstances have played out before my eyes. Hence the title of the book 'Just when you think you're winning' This next chapter throws up another surprising end.

This is a type of incident that I was often called to and it involves a 'trapped criminal.' This is when negotiators are called out to a person who is trying to escape a crime in action, but then the person has ended up trapped at the scene. This is usually because a cop has managed to catch them in the act or because the person lost their nerve and made a mistake in their attempt to break the law.

Predictably, these criminals are always angry with us for trapping them in situ. Some are confined in locations where they know they can't escape us. They usually only decide to give up their position when their basic needs require addressing, for example, the desire to urinate or eat outweighs their desire to not get arrested. Only then will they get down from wherever it is that they're perched or come out of the place where they are holed up.

One of the first cases of entrapment to which I was involved occurred on the flat level roof of a school building one Sunday afternoon. I arrived at the scene in the allocated traffic car and approached the negotiator coordinator to ask her what was happening.

'He was caught burgling the school' she told me. 'And when he tried to escape, he was stopped by the local police. He climbed on to the roof' (she indicated to a small outbuilding only a few metres away) 'and now he won't come down. We think he might have gone to sleep.'

Sleep? Oh great, I think to myself, he must be really stressed and worried about his current situation then.

We set about doing a scout of the building to see if it would be feasible to join 'Mr concerned' on the roof to ask him politely if he'd like to come down. After a quick walk around however, it was quite clear that our plan to get on the roof was not going to be easy.

Our chap had broken off the downpipes that he'd used to scale the building, which made any new access to the roof impossible. If we were to place a ladder against the wall of the building, he could easily push it away. So, as it was only two storeys high, we decided that our best course of action would be to shout up from the street. The building itself was located in a residential area and since it was a Sunday we would be disturbing the local residents by shouting, which is not helpful.

Unfortunately, our inability to physically join him made our attempt at building rapport slightly more difficult. (It's always hard to build a relationship with someone who is two storeys higher up than you on a roof and asleep).

I positioned myself a little way down the street and looked up onto the roof. I managed to spy a young man of about twenty-five years old, lying flat on his stomach, head turned away. He was either sleeping or dead and I couldn't be sure which. The following dialogue began.

M. (Shouting) Hello? Hello? My name is Martin. I am here as I want you to come down safely. I will ensure that you are looked after.

(No answer).

M. Hello? What's your name?

(Silence).

M. Hello? It's in your interest to chat to me as I can help you come down safely and make sure you know all the facts regarding what's about to happen to you.

(Nothing).

M. Hello?

At this point it seemed that I was destined to speak (or rather shout) to an unresponsive dead or asleep person for quite some time. Occasionally we get into this situation where the criminal just won't respond. What do we do? We keep trying. Sometimes we have to take a break then come back. The lack of replying can be a 'saving face issue' on their part. The person feels embarrassed and doesn't want to talk about the fact that they've been caught committing a crime. In such a case, it's my job to try and build their self-esteem and avoid comments that will make them feel self-conscious or pathetic. In general, comments like *'Hey, wanker, you got caught trying to escape, I guess you're not such a clever mastermind now, are you?'* should be avoided. Well then, here we go, I thought to myself, let's build this criminal some self-esteem.

M: Look, you are important enough for us to not just leave you here. We want to help you down. We care about your safety and that's why I am here talking to you. We have a ladder, so why don't you come down and we will give you some breakfast? Sound good?

(No reply).

M: I have to be honest. We are not going away until you come down. We don't want you to fall and hurt yourself. You did very well getting up there, but you have destroyed the means to get down. We can help you.

(After a minute he responds).

Criminal. Fuck off, tosser.

(The body now sits up and stares at me through irritating little eyes).

M. Oh, you're awake.

C. Yeah because you fucking woke me up, tosser.

(Hmm. Well some response is better than nothing. Although this over used and, may I say, inaccurate word 'tosser', is slightly annoying).

M. So did you hear what I have been saying?

C. Listen, if you lot had just let me run off, I wouldn't be up here. So, you're to blame.

The guy's logical. I can't deny it.

M. That's a very interesting observation. However, if you hadn't burgled the school and had just given yourself up to the police when they tried to stop you, we wouldn't be in this position at all.

C. That's bollocks I didn't burgle any school. They were trying to stitch me up.

M. I see. Well if what you say is true, let's all go off to the station together to sort this out. I am sure you're right *(self-esteem build)* and I am sure you will be free to go, but we have to investigate, and we will supply you with a solicitor.

C. Tell you what. I will make an appointment and come and see you later.

Of course you will mate.

M. It doesn't really work like that.

C. Fuck off then.

I often wonder what goes through such a mind in this scenario. Perhaps they think that the police will get bored and go away. Perhaps they think they can stay up there forever. Perhaps they think that if they come down right away, they'll look like a criminal who hasn't tried hard enough. Perhaps they use it as a reflection period, a time to consider getting a job or whether or not they should call their mother. Or perhaps they've mentally checked out, couldn't care less and are sitting up there whiling away the hours counting sheep and composing shopping lists. Who knows? Either way I'm curious so I decide to ask.

M. I am wondering what you are thinking. Is it that you think we will go away? Or is it that you are you a bit pissed off because you got caught and now you know you've got to give up and come down?

C. I'm thinking you are a wanker and should just piss off, so I can go to sleep.

Note to self. Add this reply to my previous list of 'I wonder what goes through the mind of a person is this scenario'

M. I see. Well like I said, we'll stay here until you come down. It looks like it's going to rain soon and I'm sure you'll start to feel cold and hungry. So, let's stop that from happening and feed you breakfast and get you a warm room somewhere. How does that sound?

Yes. That should do it. Tease him with comfort. Remind him that there's a better alternative.

I remember once in a suicide intervention case, we thought it would be best to outline the facts about taking an overdose to scare the individual into seeking medical help rather than remaining where he was (standing on a bridge over the Thames and snivelling). He had allegedly taken a lot of Paracetamol. He said he wanted to die and thought the tablets would just make him fall asleep. Little did he know.

I asked the paramedic, who was on standby at the time, to tell the gentleman all the painful, crippling and gory side effects that he would soon start to experience having overdosed. That he would soon start to feel sick and possibly start vomiting. He would get severe stomach pains. That his liver would begin to fail. That it's not as simple as losing consciousness. She told him every single gory detail as he stood there stunned, simply too frightened to speak. The effect was brilliant, one minute he was standing on the bridge threatening to jump, the next he was sprinting into an ambulance, pleading with the paramedics to take him to the nearest hospital. I've never seen anyone change their mind about suicide as quickly as that man.

Anyway, back to the roof.

C. I'm going to have a nap.

M. I'm going to keep talking to you.

C. Fine. Waste your fucking time.

M. I am going to keep talking to you.

C. I'm asleep.

M. No you are not.

C. (Snoring noises)

Knob

I think it's fair to say that this guy doesn't like police very much. I think it's also fair to say that he's a bit miffed and that this has been a long morning and I want nothing more than to go and have a nice bacon roll and a cup of tea in a nearby cafe. I decide to wander over to the coordinator and suggest to her that we go for breakfast whilst the local uniform police stand nearby to secure the building. In case our snoring burglar makes a break for it. When we return thirty minutes later and suitably refreshed, the guy on the roof is lying on his back, having resumed the dead-or-asleep position. I call up to him.

M. Hello I'm back and I'm wondering if you've now had time to think?

C. (He sits up). Where did you go?

M. For a nice Sunday breakfast. I needed some food as I thought we might be here for a while. You'd mentioned that you were going back to sleep, so I went off.

C. You really are a bunch of tossers, aren't you? Fucking, fucking bunch of tossers.

He then proceeds to bend down, rip the slates from the roof and start throwing them at us.

We duck and dodge and back quickly into a nearby doorway to protect ourselves. I see that my rapport building skills are working wonders. I guess he didn't like me walking off and abandoning him in favour of breakfast. It could be a sore spot for him. He might suffer from abandonment issues for all I know.

We call for the police to provide us with some small round dustbin sized Perspex shields and then decide on our next course of action. There's no doubt that this guy is angry. He also has very poor throwing skills. He has missed everyone. What he now needs to be told is that we're going to be adding criminal damage to the roof to his charge sheet. But I can't get over to talk to him until the shields arrive for my protection, or at the very least, until he runs out of tiles to throw. Which he does eventually.

C. Oi! Copper!

I go back over. He looks a bit out of breath. Clearly he's exerted himself.

M. Yes?

C. See who's in charge now, don't ya?

M. Well I don't think what you're doing is a very good idea. It will only get you into more trouble.

C. Come up here you tosser and we'll see who the boss is, yeah?

M. Oh no, it's too dangerous for me up there. Are you going to stop throwing things, so we can chat?

C. Bring my Mum here and I will come down.

M. Your mum?

Al Capone you are not.

I've dealt with a few incidents where a person in a crisis has asked for their loved ones to be brought to the scene. This is usually because most of the people I deal with such a scenario have been young men and it's been a personal crisis over a woman. Strangely however, in all the years that I've been doing this job, I've never once had a case where a woman wanted a man brought to the scene, or where a woman was in a crisis because of a man.

Sometimes, a man who has stated that he is about to commit suicide wants his partner or ex-partner brought to the scene so that he can show her how much he loves her. They honestly believe that such a gesture is a romantic thing to do. Can you imagine it? Being brought to the scene of a crime to witness your husband/boyfriend/ex-lover up on a bridge, dangling over the traffic, whilst a police officer stands beside you saying 'See that? See how much he loves you? He's brought the whole of West London to a standstill. He's alienated thousands of commuters and he's wasted hours of police time. He's dragged you out of work and he's re-directed half of Network Rail. See that? Isn't that great? Don't you feel special?'

To be honest, we very rarely bring such a person to the scene. It makes our job harder and makes the person in a crisis act out even more. If they really want to see someone, we sometimes bring that person to the police control point and then tease the individual down from the roof/tree/bridge by telling them that we have their loved one nearby and that if they really want to see them, all they need to do is pop down to us and have a chat. We always avoid lying to people in situations like this. If we lie, the trust is broken and once the trust is broken it makes it impossible for victims to believe us negotiators in the future. If they ever do decide to try to commit suicide, again, we need them to have faith in the system that could save them. Now let's get back to the man on the roof who is keen to see his mummy.

M. What do you wish to say to her? Why do you think bringing her to the scene will help?

C. Bring her here and I will come down. She will make sure that I am treated well.

Now contrary to all what I have written above, having this guy's mother at the scene of the crime might not be such a bad idea. After all he isn't suicidal, he is just a desperate criminal. If we get a commitment from him that he'll definitely come down if she is brought to the scene, then we can use this as an opportunity to build some reciprocity. For all you budding negotiators out there, you now know it's quite a key part of the job.

M. I will see what I can do. That's another thing that I am doing for you. Perhaps it's time for you to consider doing something for me? Like not throwing stuff at us and shouting abuse? Or even thinking about coming down?

C. Wanker!

Oh well. One can only try. I approach the coordinator and suggest to her that bringing the guy's mother to the scene might move us out of the deadlock we're facing. We have a small discussion and then agree to get the local cops to make enquiries as to her location and whether she would be willing to join us. I mean, what else would she rather be doing than attending the scene of a police negotiating incident and convincing her son (of whom she must be very proud) to come down from the roof of the school?

M. So where does your mum live? And will she be in this morning?

C. You going to get her then?

M. I think that it might be a good idea. But if she is brought here, how do you see the situation progressing? What's your main reason for wanting her here?

C. To check that you lot won't beat me up or stitch me up.

M. And you'll come down if we get a ladder up to you?

C. If she checks all is good then I might, yeah.

M. Let's see what we can do. Where is she now?

C. Ring her, I will give you the number.

He searches in his phone and shouts down a mobile number. I hand it to the coordinator and off they go to the local cops to see if this poor woman is willing come down and convince her son to stop being an idiot.

M. My coordinator has the number. We will try and get your mum here for you.

Now let's pause here for a moment. I'd like to make clear that in this case, there was no real urgency. The roof was low so even if the guy decided to jump off, he wouldn't do any real harm to himself. If we manage to get hold of his mum, we can brief her and deploy her to convince her son to come down. Then we could nick him and finally all go home. He would no doubt carry on with his life of crime and learn that in the future he should not get trapped on a roof. Whilst it's common for criminals to repeat their crimes, I've never been deployed to negotiate with the same person twice. Although some of my colleagues have.

After twenty minutes I'm informed that mum (Sandra) has been contacted and is on her way, a fact that our guy on the roof seems to be pretty chuffed about. I can't think why. If my mother was coming to talk me down from the roof I was hiding on after an exchange with the police, I'd be feeling pretty bloody fearful of the consequences. I began to wonder how this hardened criminal was going to react at his mothers' arrival.

The people we sometimes bring to the crime scene are used as intermediaries. They speak directly to the person in the crisis and we act as the number two negotiator, feeding them lines and passing notes for them to say. Occasionally we'll chip in with a few positive and affirming words of encouragement.

I made my way over to the police cordon to meet Mother Sandra, a small, frail and fifty something woman wearing an intensely irate expression. I see an officer handing her a cup of tea and updating her on the situation as Sandra lights a cigarette and looks off into the distance, bored.

I go to introduce myself and outline the situation.

'Hello there, my name's Martin and I have been talking to your son. He's not very happy at the moment. He has been chased by the police after a recent burglary that we believe he is involved in. I would like you to come with me and try to persuade him to come down from the roof. I ask that you are honest with him. He will be arrested and escorted to the local police station, but he will have legal representation and you can go with him. He asked you to be here to make sure that he was fairly treated.'

There's a long pause where Sandra stares at me with a blank, lifeless expression. 'So... what do you think?' I persevere. 'Sound like a good plan?'

She stares at my forehead, grimaces, then throws her tea on the grass before shouting 'You lot are all the fucking same!'

I get the feeling that I probably shouldn't waste too much time trying to build rapport with this woman. It is clear her views were cemented long ago. So I nod and say 'Okay,' in as friendly a fashion as I can muster. She stands there puffing her cigarette and muttering angrily. I decide to try again, simply for the sake of seeming professional.

'You sound like you're quite angry with us? Can I ask why?'

She shoots me a disgusted look.

'Well, let's face it,' she says, 'The only reason I'm here is because *you* trapped him up there and *you* can't get him down.'

Again, this is pretty accurate logic. A talent in their family.

'Good point,' I say. 'But now you're here to make sure that he comes down safely and is treated fairly. Which is really very nice of you.' I'm gritting my teeth at this point, but she's so busy sucking on her cigarette, she doesn't notice.

'I think we should walk over to him and get you to persuade him to come down. It's important that you don't provoke him. Please make him feel that coming down is really his only option and that it is the right thing to do, but that we promise to look after him.'

She stares at me with a look that suggests she wants to put her cigarette out in my eye. I persevere.

'I will let you do the talking and I'll be standing right here next to you. I might prompt you whilst you're chatting to him and suggest something to say, but you know your son better than me, so you will probably know what to say to convince him.'

She continues to stare at me and puff her cigarette and show no sign of whether she's actually heard anything I've said. Then suddenly she takes a deep breath and marches towards the building.

As we arrive, we find him sitting on the edge of the roof, dangling his legs from side to side in an irritating fashion. He was like a school kid on a park bench waiting for parents pick up time. He looks down and notices me with his mum beside him.

C. Yo mum, what's up?

S. Brian, do you fucking realise what you have made me do this morning, you ungrateful little twat?

Well this is going well. She has obviously listened to my full briefing and fully digested it.

M. Sandra, not a good id-

I'm interrupted. No real surprise there. No social etiquette this family.

S. This bloke (pointing at me) wants me to be nice to you as he thinks it'll make you come down quicker. You know me better than that, Brian. I'm going to fucking kill you!

C. Listen, I am coming down! I just want you here to make sure they don't stitch me up. You know what they do.

S. Come down then, you little shit.

M. Sandra-

C. No, I'm not sure if I want to now. I don't even feel like I can trust *you*!

This is going wonderfully. My Mother intermediary has gone off script and has upset Burglar Brian to the point where he now feels convinced that he's better off where he is. I decide to take charge and take hold of Sandra's arm to escort her back to the cordon.

S. Get your hands off me.

Sandra attempts to break free and is becoming quite a handful. I hate trying to subdue women you never know what part of the body to grab, always fearful of a complaint.

C. Leave my mum alone!

S. Brian, he's assaulting me! Did you see that?

C. Yup, I am a witness mum. He's bang to rights.

Bang to rights? This is going from bad to worse. This woman was supposed to be helping but she's frigging worse than he is.

M. OK everyone, let's think about progress and the future. Brian, if you come down, we can all go to the station. Your mum can check that we're looking after you and she can write a complaint about me if she wishes.

C. When I come down there, I'm doing you for grabbing my mum.

M. Sure, whatever gets you down quickly. Come down and make sure your mum's complaint is taken seriously.

This, believe it or not, is a good angle to work with as it gives Brian a chance to save face in his situation. Years from now he can tell the story to his mates and tell them that he came down from the roof for the simple reason that he wanted to protect his mummy.

M. Come on then.

C. Fucking right, I will!

And with that he leans over the edge, bends his knees and jumps down from the roof on to the grass below. The uniform promptly run toward him and place him in cuffs. Sandra protests at police brutality and attempts to free her son. She is pushed away, falls and is spread eagled on the pavement. This infuriated Sandra beyond measure and with that she began lashing out at the officers. Forced to now deal with her, she was promptly placed under arrest. You really can't make this stuff up!

It's worth noting that the incident came to a close because the trapped criminal believed we were assaulting his mum. (Note to self, assault more intermediaries).

A desert drive to freedom

As my experience as a negotiator increased, so too did my level of training. To qualify for foreign missions around the world, you needed a specific kind of instruction, Hostile Environment Training, which I found out I was to receive on a one-week training course at a well-known military base in Hereford. This was not the usual Foreign and Commonwealth course we attended, but a pilot to see if it was more suited to our needs. We did, after all, like to think of ourselves as special.

I travelled up on a Sunday night and my induction began with me being shown to my room, which was probably one of the most disgusting places I'd ever entered. There were no windows, which immediately cast the place as dark, dull and oppressive. The mattress was covered with plastic (for reasons I didn't know and could safely say didn't want to) and the floor, which was covered with old lino, was peeling up from the corners and moulding at the sides. 'Terrific' I thought as I bent down to unzip my suitcase, 'I'm sleeping in a prison.'

I had been in there for five minutes when suddenly the door to my room burst open and a rather scary looking army type, with stocky legs and a goatee was standing in front of me wearing army fatigues and boots. I felt strangely trapped.

'Hello mate,' he grinned, 'You is from the Met I gather?' It seemed my presence on the course was already known, although being ten years older than all the other students and the only non-military student at that, it was only a matter of time before they figured out who I was.

I nodded and asked him if he was one of the instructors. 'I sure am, coppa,' he grinned again, 'and I have something that's going to keep you company.' That didn't sound promising. And why was he grinning? Assuming he meant a bunk mate. He left the room and came back a moment later with about a hundred magazines clutched to his chest. He stood in the doorway grinning, before throwing the magazines down on to the bed, where they landed face up to reveal a series of images, each more explicit than the last. On the plus side, I thought, pornos are an improvement from a housemate. I couldn't figure out why he was giving these to me. Did I look so desperate to him that I was in need of a porno to keep me company at night? Perhaps the magazines were the student's contraband, and this was all a set-up, deliberately orchestrated to get me in trouble before a surprise room inspection tomorrow. I never knew the answer as the stocky officer cast me one last grin, winked, nodded with approval and then marched off down the corridor. 'Well', I think to myself, 'if I am going to read them, I'd better lock the door.' It turns out hiding a mountain of porn in your bedroom is a lot harder than you'd think. The cleaners in the morning are sure to be gossiping about the man from London who has a sex addiction.

The start of the course was basic, low-level content, for military non-frontline staff to learn how to recognise land mines, jump between vehicles in the event of a rescue and cope as a hostage. The training days usually began with a lecture. I woke that first morning, ate a nice fry up in the canteen and made my way to a freezing hall which kind of resembled an aircraft hangar (in fact, I think it was one). There was a stage at the end and rows of hard plastic seats for us students. I always have quite high expectations of presentations, having had a fair bit of experience of delivering them in my previous roles in the police. I worked as a recruit instructor, was previously in charge of all Metropolitan Police leadership training and designed and implemented the National Police Firearms Command Training. I have learnt a lot about what separates a good presentation from a bad one.

But this presentation was like something out of the 1970's. There we were about 30 of us sat in rows in a cold hall and the instructor, who was on stage, with a huge screen projecting lots of PowerPoint slides above his head. The students that gathered around me were either dressed in a mixture of civilian clothes or a variety of military uniforms. The instructor was showing us a few carefully constructed slides, about fifty of them in all and what looked like, identical pictures of landmines.

I could see a few of the delegates rolling their eyes with their heads lolling with boredom. Suddenly, the instructor clicked the next slide and we were presented with not so much a landmine but an incredibly hairy woman, standing totally naked on a beach. 'How did that picture of the wife get in there?' the instructor chortled. I could see a few heads in the back row suddenly bolt upright, their fatigue lifted. I could see the only two female members of the audience shifting uncomfortably, their mouths strained, fake smiles stamped on their faces. If I had tried that supposed *joke* back in the Met I would have been sacked. In this environment it appears its acceptable behaviour.

It wasn't until later in the week, when I'd built up enough of a rapport with the instructor who'd given that presentation, that I gingerly approached him over a cup of coffee. 'That picture you put up with the hairy woman during the landmine guessing game...what do you think the two women in the audience thought about it?'

He looked at me with an over exaggerated confused expression, eyes wide apart and eyebrows arched up, 'Were there two women in the audience?' he asked incredulously. He knew they were there but decided to deflect my comments with more humour. Oh well, I did try.

The week continued with some good laughs and bizarre exercises. I learned how to strip an SA80 rifle. I couldn't tell you why we were taught this, as it's not a skill that police need to have. At least I could now feel safe in the knowledge that if I ever came across an advancing terrorist in North West London, I could dismantle his gun, clean it and put it back together again in a couple of minutes. So much for run, hide, fight. More like dismantle, cleanse, assemble.

On day four, our exercise involved walking into the local town and into a supermarket wearing civilian clothes whilst concealing a hand gun. The local police had been briefed beforehand and told to ignore us if we were noticed. We walked around looking as inconspicuous as three men could, walking around the meat counter with sports jackets and a gun bulging under their lapels. No one ever noticed us. Perhaps they were too busy picking discounted ham and squabbling with their children in the biscuit aisle. Again, I was not sure why we were doing this.

Relations between the training staff and the students were never relaxed, which was clear on the day before the final live shooting exercise. I was standing in a circle of fellow students, waiting for our briefing, when one of the women students spoke in a timid voice to the instructor 'Excuse me staff, but I have forgotten to bring my ballistic helmet.' The response that followed can only be described as a bit over the top. 'You fucking done what? You fucking useless piece of fucking useless shit!' He was shouting so much at this poor woman that he managed to cool down the cup of tea I was holding.

So again, I felt the need to protest for these women and address this behaviour, but who was I? I was a guest on a course that was populated solely by the military. It was a privilege to be invited, and I didn't want to make waves. That said I was intrigued as to why there was so much vitriol. I decided to leave it and accept this was the done thing. I regret this, and it is not something I am proud of.

I didn't really make any friends on this course and I sensed I was laughed at behind the scenes. I was most definitely the granddad of the group, and a cop to boot. Many of my fellow students had previous bad experiences with people from my profession and relayed countless stories of being stitched up and stopped and searched unnecessarily, because they were totally innocent. Yeah right.

On the final exercise of the program, we were to drive around the barren landscape of the camp and approach various checkpoints that were set up by staff as a role-play. The area was a couple of acres of fields and vehicle tracks with the odd copse of trees. We were to determine whether it was a real check point or a fake one manned by terrorist insurgents. The exercise was very intense and would us involve using all the training skills we'd learnt in that week. Skills included, throwing live grenades, stripping down weapons, identifying landmines, walking around Tesco's with a concealed weapon, advanced map reading and other lifesaving knowledge for Iraq war zones.

There we were, groups of three or more in each car. In my vehicle I was behind the steering wheel, all of us holding side arms loaded with blanks. Exciting! We set off slowly on the course they issued us and continually scanned our field of vision.

Not a lot happened for about five minutes, then suddenly, through the rear-view mirror I noticed that there was a car approaching at high speed. And it wasn't stopping. A moment later, I felt a shunt from behind. At this moment I remembered being told that criminals frequently perform fake accidents and that the important thing to do was stay in the car and drive to a safe haven. I kept the engine running in case of a quick getaway and gave a commentary to my fellow passengers as to what was unfolding in the mirror.

I relayed that I could see a man in a thawb approaching the car. (Strange outfit for Herefordshire). He banged on the rear offside window with his hand where one of my passengers was seated. He then began brandishing a gun which he took from the inside of his garment. In the mirror I could see the other passengers from his vehicle getting out, also armed and began approaching us. Right, I thought, let's do this! I put the car into reverse, accelerated and rammed back into their vehicle, which in turn glided back into the ditch behind it. I watched its passengers exit the vehicle and leap left and right out of harm's way. Good job, I thought, no one's hurt and now we can drive off at high speed. I was bound to get top marks for this exercise. But just as I was settling into a feeling of euphoric brilliance, I was greeted by my red-faced instructor at the car window who was out of breath and extremely angry.

'Richards! What the *fuck* did you just do? Who the fuck do you think you are, the fucking Sweeney?'

I found out later that these types of training courses (unlike the ones I'd read about) were not intended to be taken so seriously and that ramming a military establishment car into a ditch was a move that left me in nobody's good books. Good fun though.

Despite that, it was a good course that gave me some interesting insights and experience. How much it prepared me for the likes of Iraq and Afghanistan, I was yet to find out.

This is what my training boiled down to. A trip to a far-flung land in the Middle East. The case I'm about to tell you of, went on for many weeks and involved three employees being kidnapped by some rather unsavoury types of people. We were housed in the British Embassy in Afghanistan and were to sleep in what they call 'pods' – bomb proof metal rooms that looked like mini bungalows and which consisted of a single bed and sink. The terrain inside the grounds was dusty and barren, but there was a gym and a canteen.

I've always been a bit of a gym nut and love to keep in shape, but this gym left me feeling a little intimidated. As you walked towards it, all revved up and ready to go, a team of burly looking SAS types would be standing by the door. No doubt laughing inwardly at my skinny legs and less-than-rugged appearance. Intimidated, I'd nod and end up walking straight past them, making out I was going for a run instead. I never had one gym workout during the entire time I was staying there. Wimp.

The one thing to avoid in foreign climes is salad. They wash it with local water, which is usually unsanitary, so the chances of getting an upset stomach (or worse) after eating it is usually fairly high. I avoided the salad diligently and felt OK for about a week until, bam, out of nowhere; I got the most horrendous gastric bug imaginable. Being the lead negotiator with a raging upset stomach is pretty difficult to manage. You can hardly walk into a negotiating cell and say 'Hey guys! Look I'm really sorry, but I've got gastro. Could you let the kidnappers know? Tell them I'll be back in touch after a few Dioralytes.' So, I admirably walked into the negotiating cell, complained to everyone there that I was not feeling too good, which was met with shrugs and 'oh well sorry to hear that', which really meant 'and?? You got work to do, so stop moaning'

I spent 48 hours lying on the floor, shivering and aching, whilst fielding calls from keen intermediaries who wanted to talk about how they were going to help us get our hostages back home. Eventually I was able to move from the floor to a seating position in a chair. Not the most glamorous start to the process.

This case in the Middle East involved negotiating with intermediaries through an interpreter. It isn't an easy process. Understanding the intonation and nuances in another language is very difficult, but it's crucial in our line of work if we are to build real rapport with the person we're negotiating with.

Our interpreter was employed by the embassy, a lovely chap, who worked for the local police. He had been specially selected with the task of helping us negotiate to release our hostages and return them safely home. As far as worthwhile careers go, I'd say this one was up there for him.

When we select such communicators, we look for a certain skill set. An ideal person should have the following attributes: accepting of coaching, loyal, flexible in their work attitude with a knowledge of local culture and language. They must be persuasive, articulate, reliable, and calm. They need a sense of humour, a thick skin, intelligence and discipline. In other words, they have to be bloody fantastic and we rarely find such a person when we need them. Thankfully, the guy for this mission ticked most of those boxes.

A week or so went by with some progress. We managed to build rapport with two local intermediaries who were helping us pass messages to the kidnappers. Our strategy being to buy time while we gain intelligence as to the hostages' location. Each night, after a whole day negotiating or sitting in the negotiation cell, I would send my interpreter home for the night with the mobile phone and tape recorder. This was in case we had overnight contact. As he trotted off home, I issued him with a loose script so that he'd know what to say in my absence.

We'd agreed that if a contact were to happen, the interpreter would ring me from another phone and translate what he was receiving. I would then issue a reply which he would feed back to the kidnapper. A disjointed plan of action it must be said, but it was the best we could do under the circumstances. (Unless I went home with the interpreter or he slept in my pod and neither one of us were particularly keen to resort to those measures).

For three weeks we spoke with the intermediaries, we gathered intelligence and planned for contingencies. We assumed we had the scenario figured out. But that night, the interpreter received a text message.

'We have released the hostages and they are driving on their own towards you.'

The message was duly translated to me via a telephone call at 4am in the morning. At first I thought I'd dreamt it, so knackered I was from the grind of the day before. I tried taking the message in but felt immediately uneasy. What sort of kidnapper suddenly releases hostages, puts them in a car and asks them to drive *themselves* to a large city? It was the equivalent of a hostage from Afghanistan being released into the Wiltshire countryside, in the UK, placed in a car and told to drive over to Central London.

Throughout this case we'd had a few false promises from the kidnappers, an example being, that their release was imminent. We'd waited with anticipation, hoping it was true, but the release would never come. So, we'd all come to treat such information with a pinch of salt. I asked for clarification from my interpreter whilst rubbing my eyes and getting dressed at the same time. As he spoke, the information he obtained became more detailed: *'the car is a silver Toyota, released about half an hour ago, not sure where from, or the direction.'* I was less sceptical when he said the car was a Toyota. The whole country seems to drive them, and they are damn reliable after all.

But what if they got lost/ ran out of petrol/ got kidnapped again/ broke down? I didn't know who these kidnappers were, but I certainly knew they were reckless.

I pulled on my trousers, exited my metal pod and ran outside to the team sleeping next door. I knocked frantically. 'They've been released!' I shouted to the female colleague who answered the door. She was blearily rubbing her eyes and momentarily forgetting that she was wearing nothing but a long shirt and pair of knickers. It's always a shock seeing your work colleagues in their underwear, but all embarrassment goes out the window when you're faced with three vulnerable hostages driving around Afghanistan in a silver Toyota.

I immediately ran back to my pod and rang my interpreter back, asking him to give me regular updates. As I cast a glance at my reflection in the mirror, I noticed that I actually looked excited. I grabbed my paperwork and phone and walked briskly to the negotiating cell, checking my excitement and putting my relaxed game face back on. I wanted to show the others that I was chilled, that I'd dealt with hundreds of these cases before and that it really wasn't a big deal to me. I entered the cell and was shortly joined by my previously half-dressed colleague, who was now wearing a full set of clothing and a focussed expression. We paced the room, waiting for our boss whilst wondering what to do next. If we were to go out and search for this car, we would need a local escort, which we didn't have. We also didn't know where to look.

Suddenly the boss stormed into the room wearing *his* game face (seems like we all have them). He issued us with a stare before announcing 'We're off, let's get looking.' I was stunned. We weren't looking for a snot-nosed seventeen-year-old suspected car thief from a council estate in East London. We're looking for three hostages in Kabul at 4.30 a.m. and we had no idea where we were going. Still, I wasn't about to doubt my boss's decision making. I was far too excited for that. I nodded in agreement and headed off into the cold misty morning.

We walked into the yard where my boss had arranged for a driver to meet us in an SUV. I squeezed into the rear seat, sandwiched between two of my colleagues and the boss. As we began our search, I attempted to talk to my interpreter who by this point was getting so over-excited about the kidnapping coming to a close, I had to use a lot of effort to try to calm him down. I pictured him standing in his pyjamas with his wife looking on in amazement that her husband was wrapped up in such an episode.

We drove around for about half an hour and were beginning to feel despondent, when I heard a cry from my colleague in the back seat of our SUV. 'There it is!' Sure enough, as I glanced over to my left, I could see a crowd of about fifteen people standing around a silver Toyota talking in an excited manner and pointing to the occupants. Without a moments' hesitation our car screeched to a halt and we all leapt simultaneously out of the car (an embarrassing moment for me as I didn't so much jump out but *fall out*). My phone dropped to the tarmac and crumbled onto the road just as my legs gave way from under me. In truth, I'd thought the ground was closer than it actually was. I had completely forgotten that we were higher up in a 4wd SUV. How embarrassing I thought, as the crowds gathered around the Toyota, momentarily dispersed to make room for the three acrobatic policemen hurtling towards them. I could see the three hostages sitting in the car. We knew it was them because we'd been staring at their photographs for over three weeks. And now here they were, alive, and sitting in a car looking absolutely petrified.

'Open the doors' we shouted, expecting a hasty response, but all they did was sit, staring straight ahead, looking terrified. Why were they just sitting there? Didn't they want to be rescued? My logical brain was questioning this situation. Then it dawned on me that they might have thought they were being *re*-kidnapped. After all, there they were, surrounded by people they didn't know, all of which were shouting at them to get out of the car. Not only that, but one of them (me) had fallen out of the car in a comical yet heroic fashion. They probably thought we were drunk criminals looking to do some damage. Then my boss shouted, 'Police Scotland Yard' and flashed his British police warrant card ID. Unorthodox, but brilliant. Who in their right mind would shout that sentence in the centre of Kabul at 5 a.m., if they weren't the real thing? And it worked! The hostages unlocked the doors but continued to look very confused.

We quickly opened the doors and extracted our confused specimens from the car. None of them looked particularly happy or relieved to see us. Weird, I thought. Too much of an emotional overload, perhaps. We ushered the hostages into our vehicle, taking care not to get any of them clipped by the oncoming traffic. The headline *'British Police Kill Hostages in Fatal Road Traffic Accident after rescuing them'* would not look great, especially as it was my first overseas deployment and I was trying to make a good impression. We pushed them into our 4x4 and headed off towards the military hospital.

I took a backward glance at the crowd still standing around the hostage's vehicle. They were now staring at our departing makeshift rescue wagon with confusion etched across their faces. Imagine watching this in the UK and seeing some Afghani law enforcement squad dragging out some hostages from a car in Kensington and Chelsea in London. I also think that shouting 'Afghan military!' in Chelsea might get you shot, instead of being laughed at by shouting 'Scotland Yard', in Kabul.

The excitement didn't end there though.

We made our way with great speed towards the military hospital. My boss made numerous telephone calls from the front passenger seat, notifying various agencies that our hostages had been released. I was crammed in the open space in the boot, my colleague next to me, grinning from ear to ear at the good fortune of our mission. The three hostages were all crammed into the rear seat. As we were sat there, grinning like Cheshire cats in disbelief, I glanced out the rear dusty window and saw, to my surprise, a car full of thugs, big and terrifying, with a long-barrelled machine gun rotating from the top of their vehicle roof. I was stunned. It looked like a scene from a Mad Max film. Friend or foe? I didn't know and immediately panic set in. The thought that we were about to be kidnapped with a group of pre-kidnapped hostages beside us seemed very ironic, not to mention embarrassing and scary. *'Rescue Police Get Kidnapped En Route From Rescue Mission.'* That sounded even dafter than the last headline.

We pointed out to the driver that we were being followed (in a mild panicky sort of way) and prepared to take evasive action. At this point, the hostages in our car looked even more terrified, as the Mad Max lookalikes behind us started swivelling the turret of their gun towards us. Rather than stopping, we drove on at high speed, the desert dust behind us creating a comforting visual barrier between us and the whackos chasing behind. After about ten minutes of not being shot, it was confirmed to us over the phone that they were indeed friends and not foes. They had actually been responsible for helping us to safely arrive at the hospital. If only they could have carried out their support mission with a slightly less menacing appearance.

I relaxed at this point before taking in the stupidity of our decision making so far. We had been fools to leave the embassy without an escort. Fools to approach and open a car that could have been either booby-trapped or followed by the armed kidnappers. But we were successful in rescuing the hostages, who could have been retaken by the crowd that had surrounded the vehicle. Reckless we were, yet our old-fashioned British policing saved the day.

We reached the military hospital and walked the dazed hostages inside. A calm and very lovely doctor approached them, asking a few personal details. They were then escorted into private cubicles for a medical examination.

I remained at the hospital for a while, pacing around frantically, to rid my body of all the adrenaline it had stored up. I decided to ring my then wife and tell her our good news. By now, with all the excitement, I'd forgotten the time difference from the Middle East to England and rather than being congratulated, I got a few choice words in my ear for waking her up. (She never did understand my line of work, or me).

After the hostages were medically examined, fed and watered, it was decided that I was to be part of the debrief team. The importance of debriefing hostages can never be underestimated.

Its important to learn from these events so we can understand what happens in strongholds, the dynamics of the kidnappers and also train people how best to deal with such events. The more information we have, the more we can understand what really happened rather than what a hostage tells us when they are being held and made to say things over the phone, which are untruths.

Here are examples of typical questions:

Interrogation: Who was present? How was it carried out?

The release: How were the hostages made aware of the release? What messages were they given? What was the procedure of the release?

Captivity conditions: How were they fed? What were their toilet facilities like? Were clothes worn? Were they allowed to talk? How often were they moved? Did they have knowledge of their location? Did they have access to books/ radios/ home comforts?

Detention: How many guards were present? What were their rituals? Knowledge of the negotiations?

Medical: Were the hostages allowed access to medication?

During Kidnap: Were any instructions given? Were they assaulted, searched or anchored?

Relationships: What was their relationship with the other hostages? What was the mood during negotiations?

The following day I was tasked with another officer to debrief one of the three hostages. It was a difficult task as the details of their captivity were pretty horrible. This hostage believed they could identify the place they were held, because of landmarks they had seen out of a window where they were held. We were asked to drive around with UK Special Forces to try and establish this location. We were divided into two vehicles for an expedition that took all of one afternoon.

We set off, full of apprehension yet feeling positive that we would complete our mission. After an hour, we arrived at the outskirts of Kabul and drove down a deserted narrow alleyway before coming to a halt. Throughout the drive we had been in constant radio contact with the support vehicle behind us, as well as the Control Room we had left behind. The support vehicle had kept so close by; it was no more than two inches from our rear fender.

Here we were our first stop after leaving the embassy, half way along a cramped, oppressive, 200-yard-long alleyway with high walls climbing up either side of the vehicle. The dust slowly settled before we were approached by some bearded chap coming towards us on a motor bike. He knocked on the driver's window. He was dressed in robes and motorcycle boots with no helmet. He leant in, elbows resting on the window ledge and murmured to our driver. I could just make out the word 'hostage.' After lots of pointing and whispering to our driver/interpreter we were asked to drive off with our motorcyclist in tow. So off we went. After a few metres we would stop again, as the motorcyclist would approach the vehicle, whisper something, point and then again drive off. I repeatedly looked back out the rear window to see this bearded biker following us and laughing manically, with deranged wide eyes and yellowing, uneven teeth, as he fought to balance his bike on the uneven dusty roads of the alleyways.

After several more false starts, lots of leaning in, whispering and pointing I decided I'd had enough.

'What's going on?' I asked the driver impatiently.

'He is a local, with information about what we are looking for.'

'Really?' I enquire. 'What information exactly? Does he know where the hostages were being held?'

'Not really' was the reply.

'So, what's with all the pointing and whispering?'

'That's how things are done. He's trying to be discreet.'

Discreet? Really? He's following two armed 4 x4 vehicles down alleyways on a motorbike whilst cackling away like a madman. And he's trying to be discreet?

We drove around for another two hours, as the hostages almost-but-not-quite identified the premises they thought they had been held in. I say *not quite* as they recognised the buildings that they could see from the stronghold but were unable to pin point the exact window they'd looked out from. In the end, frustrated and tired, we began our return journey. We were pretty down after our search. The hostage was also. I think they felt that they had failed us in some way and that being unable to identify their location of capture had failed to give them the closure they'd so desired.

En route back to the base, we heard an urgent radio transmission between the drivers of both our vehicles. Oh no, I thought, we are at risk. I knew it! I'm going to be kidnapped by a bearded motorcycle gang wearing robes and no helmets. The two vehicles suddenly changed course, weaving in and out of the oncoming traffic. Horns were sounded and people in the car looked concerned. I immediately thought back to my hostile environment training and wondered whether I could remember how to strip down an SA80 rifle and put it back together again. The vehicles drove into a dusty car park and several armed guards jumped out of the following vehicle before coming over to us as a second driver got out. I braced myself for the attack, just as I saw the three men dive round a back of a building skip, unzip their flies…and began to relieve themselves!

Project Pissing complete, we headed back to the embassy, dejected and disappointed by the afternoons' events which had so far involved a tour of a strange city, being stalked by a crazed and toothless motorcyclist and, finally, urgent toilet breaks.

Gathering nuts in Kabul

Another one of my other earlier involvements with an international kidnap for ransom was a gruelling experience, one that contained some very bizarre moments. Several hostages had been taken by an unknown organisation. I was to be part of the negotiating team, flown out again specially to handle the situation.

The rooms set up for our overseas deployments always looked the same. One big table surrounded by hard, plastic chairs accompanied by small windows and bright, imposing fluorescent lights that cast the drab wallpaper into a more depressing shade of magnolia. It was the usual team around the table. Me, the Number One Negotiator, the Coach, the Coordinator and some guy from the Foreign and Commonwealth Office (FCO) whose name I could never remember. On the tables would be tape recorders, written prompts, spare tapes, pens, papers, spare batteries, bottles of water, all of which made up what we called the 'negotiating cell.' Entry to the room would be restricted to those with a certain level of security clearance and a real need to be in there; we needed to minimise distractions in case a call came through.

The first few days of the kidnap-for-ransom were pretty mundane. No contact was made by the kidnappers, so we spent our time preparing for any and every eventuality such as anticipating who would ring the phone and what we would say to them if they did.

We have all in the course of our lives, spent time waiting for a vitally important telephone call. Be it for a job interview, a promotion, a test score, a hospital result. We negotiators experience that same anxious feeling on jobs like these, except that our anxiety is threefold because someone's life depends on it. As you wait, you wonder what's going to be said, what the demands will be, and what tirade of abuse will be shouted at you. (This one is particularly common if the certain someone is high on drugs). Above all, you wonder what the outcome will be. Will you be able to save someone's life, or not?

As negotiators, we spend our lives waiting, writing up *dos'* and *don'ts*, rehearsing possible scripts for what we should say and flagging up the details of what should and shouldn't be discussed. We will anticipate and script most scenarios. Silence, threats to harm hostages, outrageous demands, pleading hostages.

Any available wall space in the room where we are located is filled with flip chart prompts, time lines and other useful details that we need to hand. A lot of mess is needed behind the scenes in order to pull off an A star performance.

One morning, on the third day of our routine, my boss, the coordinator, a stern looking guy of middling build and height walks into the room, looks right at me and says 'Martin, come with me.'

I follow him, feeling slightly perplexed, imagining that I was about to get in trouble for something. In the police you learn to assume the worst when your boss asks to see you in private. I quickened my pace, preparing for a tirade. He led me out of the building and into the baking hot sun. I could feel a lump beginning to form in my throat. But just as I was about to open my mouth to ask what I'd done, I saw him open the door of a parked SUV and usher me into it, its black leather seats boiling hot from the sun. He then traipsed round to the front of the car and slid into the front passenger seat, next to our driver who (I couldn't help but note) was armed for our protection.

We donned our sunglasses (obviously to look cool) and drove slowly out of the compound as the security guards waved us on our way and I nervously waited for a more detailed briefing. After a moment the boss turned to me with a smile.

'Martin,' he said, 'we're taking you to meet someone. And we want you to negotiate with him to come to the embassy and meet with us. He has made demands that are unreasonable, and he needs to be told that and we still need proof of life. If he does this, we have something to show him to demonstrate that we are serious, some cash'

I blinked in confusion, having no idea who or what he was talking about. After all, our UK policy and intention as negotiators was never to offer to pay anyone a penny. Rather than asking the *why, who, what* questions such as, *who is the person and how exactly am I meant to negotiate with them*? I simply said 'Sure' as if he'd just asked me to fetch him a loaf of bread from the supermarket.

I immediately felt out of my comfort zone. I didn't know who I was going to talk to, whether there was a covert reason for talking to them or whether it was simply a 'buying time' tactic from someone higher up in the terrorist organisation who was hoping to throw us off course. At the end of the day, this job teaches you not to ask questions. Negotiators are called mushrooms for a reason: we're kept in the dark and fed shit on a daily basis.

We drove around Kabul for about forty-five minutes, before I noticed two ornate pillars with a garish marble lion head perched on the top. They were at the entrance to a driveway that was long and winding and reminded me of a country mansion estate in Devon (except that this one was hot and dusty and in the middle of a war zone). We drive through the pillars and soon arrived outside a palatial looking building with an imposing gold and wooden fronted door.

For some hideously naïve reason, I thought my boss was staying with me for moral support but the minute my feet touched the gravel pathway outside the car, he turned to me with a smile and a 'See you later then, good luck!' before he drove off in the SUV. I watched it disappear in a cloud of dust that made my eyes water. There I was with what looked like tears running down my face, alone and nervous, with no idea of where I was or what I was supposed to be doing, other than pulling off some weird negotiation. As far as work briefs go, this one left plenty to the imagination. I wished I had asked at least one question, for example, *why?*

I pushed the huge brass doorbell and waited for up to a minute, hoping that whoever I was meeting had decided to call in sick for the afternoon. Sadly, the door was opened, and I was greeted by a pleasant enough looking young man in his twenties, wearing all white. He was standing in an ornate and high roofed entrance hall which was beautifully decorated with marble and gold leaf.

'Come in, he is waiting for you,' he said with a smile.

Who's he? Should I act dumb and ask? I considered it but instead merely replied, 'Good', with a reassuring expression that attempted to convey that I had complete comprehension as to who this 'he' actually was.

I was moving through the hallway, with my host by my side when we were suddenly met by another equally small chap, about five feet in size, who was also dressed all in white. He beamed up at me with a wonderfully kind expression and asked me if I fancied a cup of tea.

I agreed to the tea thinking it best to be polite and was then ushered into a second, more opulent hallway, which led on to an enormous, and even more opulent, gilt reception room. From the doorway I could spy a tanned bearded man sitting in a chair wearing national dress and eating a large bowl of pistachios. I began to approach him with a feigned air of confidence and even contemplated extending my hand to shake his before realising that the chap was sat there staring into space and hadn't so much as acknowledged my arrival. The two men in white slowly hovered around me, beaming pleasantly in an effort to be friendly.

The surrealism of this scenario was like something out of the Rocky Horror Picture Show. Here I was, having been greeted by the hunchbacked (or in this case, small) manservant, made to dance to the song *Time Warp* and was about to be thrown to the mercy of the lascivious, fishnet wearing transvestite. In reality though, no one in the room was wearing suspenders. Not that I could see anyway.

I walked around, admiring the furniture and surroundings which were covered with gold leaf and marble and glass. I say I admired it (my taste is more IKEA) but the surroundings felt to me, a little over the top. There are only so many marble pillars that a person needs.

My legs felt a bit wobbly as I crossed the floor, my shoes sounding like a horse on concrete as I clip-clopped along, the noise echoing around the room. I gingerly approached the formidable, nut-eating figure, assuming that he was the one who I was going to be negotiating with. I was about to extend my hand, he turned to face me, with a face of leathered skin, which looked very much like it had grown tired before its time. If I'd run in to this guy in a dark alley in central Kabul, I think it's safe to say that I would have been pretty terrified. He stared at me for what felt like a decade, taking me in and chewing me up with his eyes. He didn't say a word, he just stared and stared. *How rude*, I thought. I could only suppose that he thought himself too important to stand up. Perhaps this was his way of playing it tough and showing the Englishman with the Oakley's balanced on his forehead who was boss. (On closer reflection, wearing my Oakley's on top of my head might not have been such a great idea in this delicate situation. The last thing I'd wanted was for him to think I was trying to be cool. I needed to build respect with this guy). I decided to adopt a relaxed mood for our forthcoming battle.

'Hello,' I said, stretching out my hand. 'I'm Martin from the UK Embassy, how are you?'

'Uh,' a deep, gruff grunt was the reply. I then heard a voice over my shoulder and a sentence I didn't understand. One of the men in white was translating my introduction for me! Not only did I have to negotiate with a nasty, nut-eating, refusing-to-stand-up local, but I had to negotiate through an interpreter.

I sighed inwardly and took a seat next to the bearded wonder in the rather grand leather club chair that was pulled up beside him. It was the sort of thing you usually saw in posh hotels beside a fireplace. I paused for thought and stared at the window directly opposite. The intense sunlight was shining into my face and making me squint. Conveniently for my opponent it seemed his face was in the shade. I was however at an angle where he could see every bead of sweat that was forming on my forehead. He'd taken the upper hand on the seating plan.

At that moment the smaller manservant came back into the room, bringing with him a silver jug and a plate of neatly arranged biscuits. He knelt at my feet and poured some tea as a few nut shells whizzed rather comically over his head. The bearded one was flicking his nut cast offs into the room where they slid regally across the shiny marble floor. It was pretty poor behaviour, even if he might be the leader of a terrorist organisation.

I leant back and took in the scenario. There I was, sat next to The Bearded *wannabe* Terrorist having a cup of tea and biscuits, as a pyjama clad interpreter/servant sat at my feet. To this day, I try to think of a more surreal experience and fail miserably.

The little fellow was to be our interpreter and it was time to use my powerful 'negotiating Jedi power' on this nut eating adversary. The interpreter to my right would have to do a good job of translating my weirdly mixed up Devonian/English accent. I was tempted to throw in the word's 'pasty' 'clotted cream' and 'cream tea' merely for my own delight.

This is how the negotiation went between me and The Bearded One (identified as 'T' for Taliban-wannabe).

M. Hello there, I am pleased to meet you.

T. Your family, are they well?

M. I'm sorry?

T. Your family. Are they well?

My family? Are they well? Ha! He might have thought that he could unnerve me with that rapport building rubbish, but I knew exactly what he was up to. Then again, pleasantries are important at the start of a negotiation. As he spoke, I noticed that bits of nut were washing around in the inside of his chops like a cement mixer in the back of a lorry. So much for initial pleasantries.

T: Your family. They well?

M. They are, thank you.

Well, there we go. I decide to reciprocate on the pleasantries and ask him about his family. Do I care? Not at all. I don't even like this person who has no manners and eats with his mouth open

M. And yours?

T. They are fine. And you, my friend, your name?

M. Martin.

T: Mr Martins, I am pleased to speak with you for we have much to discuss.

Frequently, when I travel, I'm referred to as 'Mr Martins.' I once asked an African colleague what the reason was for this and he told me that Martin with an 'S' sounds to their ears, nicer and less abrupt. He also said that they found 'Martins' easier to pronounce than my last name, 'Richards.'

T. Nut?

What did he call me?

T. Nut?

Oh, I see. He was offering me a handful of nuts. The nuts he'd been guzzling down like a semi-demented monkey. As he spoke, he leant forward and drilled me with those black eyes. The sun made me hot and the flicking shells were distracting. I was also highly aware that the interpreter sitting to my right was mumbling my replies with an Arabic-Devonian accent.

T: Nut?

M. No thanks. I've just eaten.

Now let's talk business.

M. So, I have been asked to come here to explain to you that you demand is unreasonable and we would like you to come to the embassy to discuss further. You haven't proven yet that you have our people, or that you know who has them, or even that you know where they might be. If this is possible, we have finance at the embassy for you to see.

T. *Silence.*

M. Do you think that would be a good idea?

T. *Silence.*

Was he hard of hearing?

M. What can I say to show you that we are serious in further discussions?

T. Mmmmmmmm.

Another stellar negotiation Martin. You can't even persuade a man to come to a building with you.

M. I wanted to say that I am here to show you respect and to demonstrate to you that we are serious about further dialogue. What do you think?

T. Is this a trap, my friend?

M. What? No? Absolutely not, my friend.

One area of active listening that we are taught is 'mirroring' or 'reflecting' a person's speech, this can keep a conversation going without even asking a question. It can also help to reveal the person's emotions, not to mention more information. Empathy can be created between individuals when they match or repeat the emotion, intonation and rhythm in each other's voices and repeating the last word or key words from their sentence.

The technique of mirroring the last few words spoken is useful when someone is venting anger or any encounter when someone is raising their voice, being intimidating and not listening. By mirroring you are at least demonstrating that you have heard their words and it can help to you to orientate yourself, gather your thoughts, plan for a response and buy time. Noting whether the speech intonation goes up or down at the end of a sentence can indicate a desire to close or continue the dialogue.

Conversations can also be directed by choosing which words to reflect. But it's important to be flexible in the words you choose. If your choice doesn't steer the conversation in the direction you want, pick another. Here's an example. Let's say I tell you about my journey to work this morning, which goes something like this. 'I got up, had some bran flakes for breakfast, walked to the metro station, caught a train, which was really hot and stuffy inside, then walked two miles until I arrived at my destination.' If you wanted me to focus in on the *conditions of rail travel*, you might reply 'Hot and stuffy,' which might steer me to say, 'Yeah, it was, there were no windows or air-conditioning.' Or I might reply, 'Yes, the state of the trains is getting worse in this country.' The point is, to repeat a part of the dialogue that you want the person to remain focussed on. This is a good tactic to use with suicidal people when we identify hooks and need the person to talk about them.

There we were, sitting in our big leather chairs and making zero progress on the negotiation. I was beginning to worry that I was out of my depth. I was also thinking about what would happen if I was kidnapped. I had no protection. I suddenly realised that I was here in a Rocky Horror set with three men I didn't know, who could, for all I know, be drugging my cups of tea and biscuits before planning my abduction.

I thought to myself. Would my boss have left me here without a proper risk assessment? To do such a job properly I would expect that he'd have checked to see what sort of people were in this building, their mood, and their numbers. The actual location I was in would have been researched by intelligence analysts. They would have found out whether there were any community tensions, what the crime rates were and if there were any hazards. They would know if the place was detrimental to my health or whether I was at risk of infection or injury. When deploying me he also would have considered the circumstances that could cause harm, the possibility of harm occurring, the severity of harm that could ensue and above all what measures could be implemented to mitigate that harm from happening...wouldn't he?

T. We have a problem with this. I have people to answer to.

Don't we all, mate.

M. I'm sorry to hear that. Maybe you can convince those people that we are serious. What do you think?

T. What authority do you have? Why have they sent you?

Who knows, desperation? Because I'm great? Because I was the only one in the room when they happened to be looking for volunteers?

M. I have the authority to...so you know we are serious...I was selected to speak with you because of this authority that I have.

Oh dear, here we go again, talking bollocks.

T. We are powerful people and have influence and control over many areas.

M. OK.

T. And I am trusted to make big decisions.

M. OK.

T. I am respected amongst my tribe.

M. OK.

We seemed to be at the 'ego stroking' stage of the negotiation. Interestingly, many of our kidnappers have an ego issue and feel the need to be in control. The job for me here is to feed that ego.

M. It sounds to me like you are certainly the man for me to be dealing with here. I can see why you have been asked to come here to talk with me. Your influence will be helpful to us.

Sometimes I admire my own bullshit.

T. Mr Martins. I am not sure you heard me right.

He leant towards me and was inches from my face at this point, gripping the side of his chair tightly. I could see the whites of his knuckles protruding through the skin.

T. I said I was respected and trusted. And that means I get what I want.

Suddenly we found ourselves interrupted by the gentlemen who had been kneeling down at our feet and serving us biscuits. He had returned with yet more tea and even more biscuits.

M. Why, thank you.

Despite the stressful work environment, I was beginning to get used to having a friendly manservant who brings food and drink on a regular basis.

M. So we seem to be at loggerheads.

T. What is this 'loggerheads?'

M. We can't seem to reach an agreement at present, your demands have been unreasonable, so I have been told.

T. No *you* can't.

M. *We* can't.

I sensed that I was becoming argumentative. I paused and took a moment.

M. What would it require for you to move towards my suggestion of further chats? We need proof and you want money, let us demonstrate to you our commitment.

There was the sound of crunching as The Bearded One pushed several homemade biscuits into his mouth. He seemed to never stop eating. He swallowed and made no answer. I tried again.

M. Is there something we can do to reassure you? Is there something that would make you happier with my offer or convince you of our commitment to it?

T. No.

That seemed like the perfect time to implement my Jedi mind control negotiating. I thought long and hard about a strategy that would break us out of this impasse.

M. Why not?

T. Mr Martins, you seem to not be understanding me. I need what I want. You offer an insult to all of us.

M. May I have a nut?

T. Of course.

He dipped his very grubby, dirty hand into his paper bag of nuts. He felt around for a few seconds, no doubt to make sure that he had contaminated every single one of them, before pulling his hand out and dropping a couple of sweaty nuts into my palm. I had no intention of eating it. Instead I held out my hand and positioned it under his nose. I then pointed to the nut that was resting in my left palm.

M. Imagine that this nut is our agreement. We can't get to it because of the hard shell that surrounds it. We need to find a way to crack this shell and both eat the nut.

He looked at me with total confusion.

T. I don't want snacks!

Damn. Clearly the metaphor had gotten lost in translation. Either that or he was being sarcastic, a skill that we at the Metropolitan Police know all too well. But I was not giving up on my nut analogy, so I tried again.

M. The nut is the agreement. The shell is our disagreement. We find a hammer, that is our compromise, and we shatter the shell to give you the nut.

T. Ah! I see! Yes, yes. I will have two million dollars of nuts, yes?

Was this some sort of weird Taliban humour? If so, I wasn't laughing.

M. OK. Forget the nuts. I really want to sort this out with you. I think you are an intelligent man, a respected man, an insightful man. You have the ability to do great things. An intelligent, great thing to do, that will earn you respect with your peers and show them that you have great insight, is to move matters forward with us and continue our dialogue.

T. You are trying to seduce me by paying me compliments. I cannot be fooled. You also are an intelligent man so respect me and offer me what we have asked for.

I decide to sit in silence for a while. It was very hot and airless, and I was getting tired. I was also, clearly, not getting anywhere and the situation was proving difficult to crack. Unless he were to drop dead from a nut allergy. I didn't see the negotiation coming to a successful conclusion here. I wanted to do well and return having accomplished something. But how? He continued to nibble his nuts, the pistachio shells growing into an ever-greater pile as we sat there staring at each other, neither one of us saying a word. I noticed that he never blinked, only smirked occasionally. I tried to match his unblinking persona, but I could feel my eyes watering from an accumulation of the room's dust.

T. You seem very upset Mr Martins. It's a weakness to cry during negotiations.

M. Oh no, it's the dust in here, that's all.

T. Of course.

Now he thinks he's made me cry. Bastard! It's the dust!

T. Now let's talk about how I come with you.

A moment of progress! I wasn't sure where this sudden surge of generosity came from. Perhaps he felt sorry for me because he thought he'd made me cry. Perhaps crying should be a negotiating tactic after all.

M. You will come to the embassy?

T. And?

M. You can then see that we are serious about negotiating. We will also need proof that our people are alive.

This is certainly progress. He is talking about the logistics of how to move things forward.

T. What is it you require?

M. To speak with the hostages and ask them a question that only they know the answer to.

T. What, like when did they last go to the toilet?

M. Not quite as we don't know the answer to that.

T. No they do. So they would be alive.

I don't think this guy fully understands the concept of 'proof of life.'

M. We ask you to ask him a question that only he knows the answer to, like 'What is the name of your dog?' You tell us the answer and, if it's correct, we know that he must have told you and that he must be alive.

T. Do they have a dog?

M. I don't know.

T. Then why ask this question?

Where's a brick wall when you need to beat your head against something?

M. It was just an example.

T. So I ask him his dog's name, he gives answer to me, I tell you.

M. Yes.

T. OK, so ask me the question about the dog.

M. That's not the question. That was an example. We have some questions back at the Embassy.

T. Do you have a dog, Mr Martins?

M. What?

T. A dog. Do you have a dog?

M. No.

T. Then you are dead. Ha!

Wow. Hilarious. I sensed that The Bearded One wasn't the sharpest tool in the toolbox. Either that or he was taking the mick out of me. Or he just had a really poor sense of humour. Who cared at that point? He was talking and feeling in control, which were both positives in my eyes.

T. So are we now eating this nut and coming to a deal, Mr Martins?

At this point my phone started to ring rather noisily in my pocket. I slowly took it out, making it clear that it was a mobile. The last thing I wanted was for my friend to think that I was pulling out a Glock 17 and creating a diplomatic incident. I also didn't want him to think that I was taping our conversation. I held it out for him to see and I said 'phone' really loudly so that he knew it wasn't a gun. I answered the call.

B. Hey Martin

It was the boss. I had to sound confident, like progress was being made and that I was doing a great job. I stood up and walked away from the leather club chairs so that my adversary couldn't overhear the lies that were about to spill out of my mouth.

M. Hello guv.

B. How's it going?

M. Oh, you know.

B. No, I don't.

M. Slow.

B. Well no pressure but we are all waiting here and assuming that you have built rapport and he is eating out of your hand.

Assume all you like, mate. Also my hands are not big enough to contain the amount of food he munches.

M. OK.

B. OK what?

Now it's hard to talk freely when some Taliban-wannabe chap is only a few feet away staring at you. He'd heard the words 'Slow' and 'Oh you know.' Perhaps I'd already given him a clue as to our progress. I smiled in his direction, nervously pretending that the call wasn't connected to the negotiation.

M. I will call you back.

As I made to hang up, the boss said-

B. We are coming to get you.

Clearly time was pressing. I didn't want to appear rushed after getting off the call or my nutcracker friend would realise that the situation had changed. I had to carry on acting nonchalant.

M. That was my boss. He wants to know what progress we have made. What shall we tell him when he arrives?

It's often a good idea to try to summarise the situation with the kidnapper in this way. It allows the other person to use their wording, which in turn helps their concentration. Summarising also allows you the negotiator to fill in the gaps. By re-focussing the speaker's attention, you buy yourself thinking time. It assists your comprehension and gives the speaker the opportunity to confirm or contradict your understanding. It also proves that you are interested in and listening to the other person. Unfortunately, in this case there wasn't all that much to summarise as hardly anything had happened. But I let him speak anyway.

M. What should I tell him?

T. That we talked about nuts and dogs, and you started to cry.

M. Good, so not a lot then.

T. Tell me Mr Martins, are you what they call a negotiator?

M. I suppose so, yes-

T. And you are trained in this field?

M. I have received some-

T. And they send you to convince me of things?

That was the third time he'd interrupted me. One of the most common mistakes people make when negotiating is interrupting the person they're meant to be negotiating with. It demonstrates that you are not interested in what they're saying and it also shows a lack of respect.

M. I am hoping to.

T. And so why-

I bring his interruption to a halt.

M. Why the questions?

T. I have seen your Denzel Washington films. *'Man on Fire'* and *'Proof of Life.'* Where is your gun?

A good question. This also posed a dilemma. If I told him I had a weapon on me then the temperature of our conversation would change entirely. If I'd told him I wasn't armed, he could have called his friends in and had me kidnapped. I thought quickly.

M. Guns don't assist with negotiation.

Crikey. I sounded like Bruce Lee in 'Enter the Dragon.'

T. Well they have helped me convince people I'm right and that people should accept what I say, especially when I've pointed it at their head.

M. Good point. Well I hope that's not the plan today.

I gave him a nervous smile. He smiled back at me and took some more nuts, then stared at me again. I tried to resume my non-blinking status but was worried that my eyes would start watering again. I went back to blinking. This is after all, a normal human thing to do.

M. Right. My boss is coming soon, so it would be good to reach an agreement before then.

T. Ah, the nut thing and the dog questions.

M. Indeed. How about we agree that you come with us, supply us with proof of life and then we go from there? I give you some questions to ask the hostages, you supply the right answers and then we are both making lots of progress. This will show trust on both sides and then we can come to a safe outcome.

T. Indeed. You give me all I ask for, I then ask the questions and we make progress.

M. Ah, you see, that is the wrong order my friend. It's ask the questions and give the right answers. Then we talk about what you want.

I'd like to point out that at no point in our conversation had I agreed to give him anything. I began to wonder if he had noticed that subtle use of my language.

T. I notice you never say you will give me anything. Mr Martins, why is this?

Bugger.

M. One stage at a time my friend. Firstly, you must prove that you have knowledge of our people.

T. Mr Martins...

He was clearly about to say something profound. I watched him carefully as he paused for effect, his mouth open.

T. The time has come to share some insight with you. I come from a land of trust, tribal ties and much conflict. Our people have seen how the West operates. How it negotiates and how it breaks promises. Invades, takes, punishes those who have different views. They doctor intelligence reports to suit their own needs and wishes whilst expecting those in countries like mine to give them grace and platitudes when asked. You expect me to give you back your people after your country has slaughtered so many of our own? Take, take, take, my friend. Then your special forces find your people, rescue them and I get forgotten and maybe detained later in your Guantanamo Bay. Wear your orange suit for fifteen years. Tell me, Mr Martins, why would anyone give you what you want? Or even believe you?

I stared back at him, slightly stunned. I couldn't think of a reply. I also felt strangely sorry for him, like I understood his cause for the very first time. But our session together was drawing to a close and my boss was about to come in and see what little progress I had made.

Suddenly we heard a crash. The door to the room was flung open and my boss appeared, having been let in by the servant. He looked flustered and hot.

B. Hello, Martin. Are we ready to go with our friend?

M. Yes, I think we are.

You liar Martin! I looked at The Bearded One, my eyebrows raised, hoping that he would agree. Not a chance.

T. I think we need some more detail.

B. Well get in the car with us and we will show you the detail. I think you will like to see it at the embassy.

There was a moment's pause before The Bearded One smiled and winked at me.

T. Fine.

And that was that. I'd spent hours trying to convince this nut job to accept my offer and my boss had managed to do it in ten seconds with no greater offer than a lift to the embassy.

The result of this case was a successful one and all the hostages were released by their captors. The the UKs government policy in such kidnappings is 'no concessions' which is well documented and means, no release of prisoners, no change in government policy and no payment for the release of its citizens.

Negotiations in such cases are therefore very difficult as we have little to offer and expectations have to be managed at an early stage. The rights and wrongs of this stance against kidnapping have been well documented and there are clear arguments for and against it. As negotiators we work within whatever policy the victims' host government adheres too. In the private and commercial world it is no different, we merely work to the wishes of the family or company concerned. We are not decision makers for very good reasons and we are not employed to question policy. We are a tactical arm; one which is deployed to operate objectively and independently in the event of a crisis. Sometimes that operation takes hours of ego massaging and nut-munching. Sometimes, frustratingly, it only takes a free trip to the embassy.

A Happy Christmas in Iraq

I travelled to Iraq on several occasions between 2004 to 2007. It was the height of the post war on terror and the American led invasion. This made these visits all the more poignant as one remembered the mass of British lives lost through kidnapping and torture. Shocking events that were often published as video footage on Al Jazeera and the like.

During these frequent trips, the comfort levels of the journey from London to Baghdad decreased. From commencing in the business class lounge of London Heathrow, followed by a nice business class flight to Kuwait, to a military transport flight from Kuwait to Baghdad before finally being taken in a Puma military Helicopter from Baghdad airport to the green zone.

To ensure that you were experienced and competent enough to represent the UK on these missions, all negotiators had to show proof of having worked within a team on an international kidnapping case as well as being experienced in attending government meetings within the Cabinet Office Briefing Room A, COBRA. These were meetings that the UK government ministers attended when the country was gripped by a crisis of some sort.

When working on the London side of these kidnappings we would assist those deployed in the country by following up on intelligence leads through special branch and anti-terrorist departments. We would also meet as a group to assist with position papers and negotiation strategies. The latter was a little counterproductive at times, because if you put a group of negotiators into a room together, odds are they'd never agree on anything. The problem being we are all trying to convince the others that our idea is the best. Never negotiate with a negotiator.

To get to Iraq I would fly to Kuwait and be met by a government representative outside Starbucks in the Arrivals terminal. I remember asking my supervisor how on Earth the representative would know what I looked like. 'He will,' was the reply. I remained unconvinced. Yet sure enough on arrival, I was plucked from the Starbucks crowd by a shifty looking gentleman with an unshaven and suntanned face.

'You FCO, mate?'

'Might be, who's asking?' was my reply. After a few *'I'm not telling you who I am unless you tell me who you are'* exchanges, we agreed to take the risk and tell each other who we each were. (Though I seem to remember that he revealed his identity first, which means I won).

As we went through arrivals, the gentleman told me that we had to drive to another airport where we would be transported via military aircraft to Baghdad. After a quick latte we jumped into a Toyota 4x4 and were escorted to a military airbase where I was told to wait until my flight. In five hours' time! There I was, the only civilian amongst a bunch of troops(again) for as far as the eye could see.

The military airbase was about the size of a football pitch and was in the middle of nowhere. It was surrounded by a high fence and consisted only of two marquee style tents and a porta-cabin which was used by military staff to check your passport, body armour and process your Thompson's holiday rental vouchers.

After they'd checked my paperwork and checked me onto the flight, I was free to walk around the camp. I looked around for some entertainment and soon found the only source of it; a group of military personal in a marquee watching lame DVDs and drinking warm bottled water. Not quite Terminal 5 at Heathrow.

I took many a journey over to Iraq by this method but will always remember one particular journey in the Hercules military aircraft. At the time I was on my own with a handful of military men in the rear cargo section of the plane. I was sat on a canvass seat in what resembled a huge aircraft hangar. I was informed that we would be picking up some troops in Basra en route to our destination. The take-off was uneventful, and I remember feeling disappointed that I wasn't offered any warm nuts or orange juice. In fact, the only contact I'd had from the air crew was from a loadmaster advising me to sit on my body armour in case anyone tried to shoot up at us through the fuselage. That makes a nice addition to 'fasten your seat belts.'

We were an hour into the journey and I was sitting there daydreaming wondering when the movie would be shown, when I felt a small shudder move through the plane which I immediately put down to turbulence. Only a minute later however the pilot came through on the radio telling us that we had to turn back to adjust the aircraft. *'Adjust what'?* I thought. The captain's seating position? And why do we need to *go back* to adjust it? Why can't we do it from up here? Or at the very least finish our flight and adjust the aircraft at our destination? I wasn't one to argue with the captain, so we turned around, flew back to Kuwait and landed safely right back where we started. I was told to stay where I was. About an hour later the pilot came over the tannoy again. He apologised for the inconvenience in our journey and told us that as that the countermeasures were showing as offline, so he'd now have to reboot the aircraft. I chuckled at that. How do you 'reboot' an aircraft? By pressing Control, Alt, Delete at the exact same time I suppose. To anyone who might be scratching their heads at this point, countermeasures are chaff. Modern armed forces use this to distract radar-guided missiles from their targets. Most military aircraft and warships have chaff dispensing systems for self-defence. The aircraft fires this out to prevent missiles hitting the plane. Quite a useful piece of kit where we were flying too, so I was all in favour of a reboot and even extra chaff please.

We all sat in the rear of the plane being told to remain where we were as it wouldn't take long. I sat in a huge cargo area waiting for someone from the IT department to *reboot* our plane. (If it's anything like our IT department they will just swan up and say to the pilot 'have you tried turning it off and on? 'Yes mate we turned it all off at 32000 feet mid-flight, but nothing happened other than we just fell out the sky').

We sat there waiting for our aircraft to be rebooted as the lights flicked on and off before it all suddenly whirred back to life. We were off again!

A few hours later several thousand feet up and still no movie, or meal, or nuts we were approaching Basra. As I felt our descent, I put away my headphones and took out my ear defenders to pay attention to the trees and tarmac below. What I didn't expect though, was that without warning I felt a 'whoosh!' as the plane tilted and we began vertical climbing at an alarming speed with plenty of bangs and bumps on either side of the plane. Scared? yes, confused? yes, crying? nearly. Its times like these that I often regretted volunteering for these postings. I began to feel sick and my stomach was in knots. I didn't have a clue what was going on. There was no warning, no tannoy explanation, nothing. Then it all went quiet, very serene, we levelled out and attempted to land again without so much as an explanation from the control deck about what was happening.

When we arrived on the tarmac my legs were still shaking and I vowed never to complain about air turbulence on domestic flights again. We were led off the tarmac to allow some very dusty troops to board. I decided to walk around to grab some air and dissipate the adrenaline. I approached one of the ground crew who was busy with large canvass straps and chains. 'So, what was that theme park type manoeuvre about then?' He replied, 'they thought that a rocket was locked onto you.' I acted cool and said, 'oh was that all, ha, good job we rebooted then.' And I nod sagely in his direction smiling with relief. He just looked confused and got on with his work and after about an hour we re-boarded. The troops were so covered with dust and sand I could barely make out their features. Hell, there was enough sand on them to make some pretty good castles. Luckily the following journey was uneventful and about an hour later we landed at Baghdad Airport. I went to grab my luggage, which was by now in its ripped and battered state looking nothing like luggage at all. I dragged it down a ramp and towards a hanger in which I would be waiting until a helicopter arrived to take us into the secure Green Zone. These Pumas are flown in pairs at a relatively low height over Baghdad's red zone. This is to ensure they don't get hit, they often chuck out a few necessary countermeasures, and dart around as they fly to avoid missiles and bullets. Before helicopters were used all these journeys were done by road. But insurgents soon got to know the routes meaning that road travel became too dangerous and we had to resort to flying. Thankfully our waiting area was slightly more luxurious than Kuwait, involving tea and coffee and even (gasp) padded chairs.

Eventually the helicopters arrived. We waited for our names to be called and walked with our wrecked luggage in orderly single file to the waiting Pumas. About ten people crammed in each one and we strapped ourselves in ready for the exciting twenty-minute journey. Off we took, and sure enough it was exciting. The side doors were open to allow a machine gunner to alternate between the openings and point his very large machine gun out into the sky and down to the streets below. What exactly he thought he was aiming at I don't quite know; we were so high up and going so fast, the houses were a mere blur, but I guess it made him feel important and reassured us somewhat. The other passengers were embassy staff and foreign office employees. We all looked apprehensive and out of our comfort zones, but also excited.

We landed twenty minutes later after zig zagging over the Red Zone and with our gunner jumping from door to door pointing his large weapon. The area we landed in looked like a car park and we were amongst some cool looking Black Hawk helicopters, which seemed a lot sexier than the beaten up one we were riding in. After waiting in the compound for a short time a guy in army uniform came over to us and beckoned for me to follow him into a white Toyota SUV. I didn't like the way he handled my suitcase, so I decided I didn't like him.

Wasting no time, we drove quickly through the streets of Baghdad before approaching the security gates of the British Embassy. Passes were shown, questions were answered and we drove up a narrow passageway hemmed in by large concrete T walls to the main reception entrance steps and exited the vehicle. We'd finally arrived. It felt like I'd left London three weeks ago. I had been in a taxi, train, plane, car, plane, helicopter, car and finally arrived. And now it was time to get to work, although at that point all I felt like was a shower, beer and bed.

On arrival at the embassy we were told that we had to attend a briefing from a security guard. We were ushered into a small room next to the entrance to await our briefing. The content of this briefing consisted of us being told where the best hiding places would be on campus in case of a mortar attack, which alarm buttons we should push, when to wear our body armour and ballistic helmets and not under any circumstances swim in the swimming pool if the security coding informed us not to. The entire briefing went on for an hour. Truth be told I hadn't thought it was possible that one embassy could have so many do's and don'ts. I came away having forgotten everything I was told, rubbing my eyes with fatigue and wondering where the pool was. It turned out that sadly it was off limits for the afternoon due to the mortars and bullets falling from the sky into the embassy grounds. We spent the rest of the evening walking around in ballistic helmets and body armour due to the heightened danger. Not sure why they told us the pool was closed as you would just sink to the bottom in all this kit anyway.

With swim time cancelled, the security guard handed each of us a map of the estate with different colour coded levels of risk and our actions for each. He informed us of our meal times and then finally showed us to our pods. They were small square rooms with a bed, table, sink and shower. The building of my accommodation was a single storeyed bungalow made of metal (Similar to Afghanistan) with sandbags lining the walls and roof for protection. I dumped my stuff in a corner and lay on my bed. I looked at my battered suitcase and wondered whether my home bought jar of marmite had survived the turbulent air travel. Suddenly there was a knock at my door. I opened it to find Mark my colleague who I was there to replace, standing in front of me. He had been out here for weeks already managing the case and looked fairly chilled out, all things considered. He had a blue folder under his arm and, to my great delight, two bottles of ice-cold lager.

'Hello mate,' he grinned. 'I'm off home in the morning so thought I'd come and brief you with some supplies.'

Before I'd left for these sunny climes I had read in on the case as much as I could. But I still needed to know what else had unfolded as there was information to be told which couldn't be shared on regular telephones.

'The Ambassador's a lovely bloke,' Mark began. 'The staff are friendly. Don't expect to use the pool though as everyday we're being fired at with mortars.' He opened our beers and we chinked them together before starting the official briefing which lasted about two hours and continued into the resident's bar. I was already beginning to get a little stir crazy in my tiny, metal accommodation. After another few drinks I was beginning to fall asleep, I was exhausted after the day's travel.

The next day I woke up full of nervous anticipation. It had been very busy over the last couple of days with new lines of communication being opened and new pieces of information that needed to be evaluated. I wondered how would I cope with my first day? I had big shoes to fill as I was taking over from Mark who was a seriously talented and experienced negotiator. I got dressed into my best Iraqi looking attire, which consisted of beige trousers and a blue shirt that had escaped the unfortunate Marmite explosion in my suitcase.

I'll never forget the first time I was walking to a meeting with the UK Ambassador. I had my blue folder in my hand, my ballistic helmet on my head. I was dreaming about home and what on earth I was supposed to say at the meeting I was heading to. Suddenly, with an unprecedented 'umph!' I was tackled into an above ground concrete bunker by one of the Gurkha guards as mortars rained over us. That was certainly the first time that I'd nearly been killed on the way to a business meeting. After a few moments of lying face down in the dirt, the guard gave the all clear and I was helped to my feet. I dusted off my trousers, feeling even more nervous than I had before. Those of you who know me as a cocky, arrogant individual might find it hard to believe that I can experience real nerves, but hey, it happens even to the best of us.

At times like these I find it helps to take a quick dip into your reserves of self-esteem and remind yourself that the reason for your presence in such a situation, is that someone important believes in you and thinks you have the ability to carry out the task at hand. I firmly believe that if you have strong leadership skills, you can get by in almost any crisis incident.

At one time in my police career I was responsible for all management and leadership training in the Metropolitan Police. I have led; small teams, large teams, surveillance teams, firearms teams, riot teams, training teams, community teams and equally been led by countless supervisors. Leadership skills have been written about by just about anyone who has a view on the subject and each has a view on what makes a *great* leader. You only have to go on LinkedIn to see a daily post on what makes a good leader and what true leadership is. Criteria I have read includes; capability, confidence, decision making ability, effective communication, fairness, innovation, integrity, fairness, and on and on it goes. All these basic skills are clearly needed, but when I look back at all *my* past supervisors, the ones that stand out for me are the people that had charisma. So as the debate continues as to whether good leaders are born with innate ability or whether this skill has to be taught. For what it's worth, I say it's a bit of both. But unless you have gravitas and charisma you will never aspire to be a *great* leader. (But what do I know).

So, if you are a leader and have charisma and possess all these wonderful skills (in other words, you're bloody perfect) then you'll be laughing through any situation that life throws at you.

My first meeting with the Ambassador was going be streamed live to COBRA in London. Waiting there to listen to my pearls of wisdom would be government ministers and key intelligence chiefs, all keen to hear what progress I had made since my arrival a mere twelve hours ago. (I could save them the time in attending the meeting). Other than yesterday's briefing and my walking to this meeting under mortar fire, not a lot had happened. I hastily read the handover sheet, which had written suggestions for future lines of enquiry. I decided that I would put those ideas forward and just nod sagely. If things got really desperate, I would nod some more and look thoughtful. If that failed I would just bullshit.

I walk into the meeting room where I was confronted by the UK Ambassador and his formidable looking team; they all looked so tense and tight-lipped sitting around the conference table. I introduced myself as the man now leading the negotiation team in the country and that I was looking forward to a swift and safe conclusion to the situation. I was asked what lines of enquiry we would now be following and the merits of my recommendations and rationale. I must have sounded and looked pretty confident as no one challenged my suggestions. We sat around the table and called via video to London. We soon connected to Whitehall where I saw lots of important men and women in suits, as well as a couple of Met policemen who I recognised. It was nice to see a few familiar faces amongst the strangers. At the very least if I said something stupid (which was likely) they'd probably jump in to support me. There then followed lots of briefings and updates about what each side of the business had been doing, which was then followed by people asking fairly repetitive and pointless questions.

I was always advised that as a meeting participant I should adhere to certain rules. It's a shame however that I have attended very few meetings where people comply with this advice. Its basic politeness really, no individual discussion, adhere to time allocations, stick to the agenda, display courtesy and avoid interruptions.

The British Ambassador who chaired the meeting was absolutely outstanding. A meeting won't be successful if everyone is pulling in different directions. He assured that everyone had an opportunity to participate. I noticed that people contributed properly and participated actively. He was impartial and stuck to the facts. No one was allowed to stray from the point and he kept his hands on the wheel. What was also encouraging was the manner in which he included all those that were present, and that each member of the meeting had the ability to contribute freely without being interrupted or ignored. He exhausted the supply of ideas before evaluating, comparing and making decisions. Finally, he checked around the group for consensus and comprehension before finalizing decisions to give the participants ownership. Fantastic! Behaviour rarely exhibited by a meeting chairperson.

After the first meeting with London I was feeling more confident and had managed to convince myself that I actually knew what I was doing. My internal mantra was working. After all, someone must have believed in me to have sent me here and if all else failed; I would fall back on my generic leadership ability (Bullshit).

One of these visits to Iraq was particularly testing for me as it happened to fall over Christmas. It also must have been one of the strangest Christmas mornings anyone had ever experienced. This time around I was sharing a double pod with a colleague of mine called Stephen. (You remember the depressed flight companion of earlier). This chap could snore for England and spent so long in the bathroom every morning one would think he was re-tiling it. At 7 a.m. on Christmas morning I was woken by an alarm sounding and whistling that could be heard coming from outside our palatial accommodation. That could only mean one thing, missile warning! I leapt out of bed and immediately crawled under it, whilst simultaneously grabbing my body armour and helmet. As I lay in the gathering dust beneath my metal bed, I looked across the room and saw Stephen in the same position. We stared at each other in disbelief as we waited and hoped for the all-clear.

As I lay there, I remembered all the other Christmas mornings that I'd experienced in my life time. All exciting (a bit like this one), all full of surprises (a bit like this one) and all with an expectation of what happiness the day would bring (not quite like this one).

After about ten minutes the all-clear came and we both stood up, exchanged Happy Christmas's as we dusted ourselves down. What next, I thought. Then as if by magic there was a loud knock at the door. I opened it only to be greeted by an elf, driving a golf cart and sitting next to a Santa Claus decked out in red velvet holding a tray of Bucks Fizz.

'Ho, ho, ho! Happy Christmas,' said the Santa, who looked rather a lot like a disguised embassy employee to me. He handed each of us a Bucks Fizz before driving off down the path to knock on the door of the next pod. You can't make this stuff up, really.

I closed the door and Stephen and I made a toast to the day ahead. I found myself thinking about the hostages out there, desperate to get home to their loved ones. It always helps to remind yourself of why you're out there doing this job.

As the day unfolded, all the embassy staff worked hard to make the place feel like home for us. There was the traditional big roast lunch with crackers and a tree, all served up by embassy workers in fancy dress. They even had numerous sporting activities on offer like tennis and volleyball. It wasn't quite the same as being home and I found it hard being away from my loved ones at that time of year. I tried to stop being selfish and keep reminding myself of why I was out there.

Christmas Day came and went without any contact from our kidnappers. We held the usual 'update' meetings in the evening and attempted to evaluate the information we'd obtained during the day. When doing this we use a tried and tested system and it's important to stress the difference between information and intelligence. *Information* is raw data and *intelligence* is an evaluation of it.

A source that has supplied sound information in the past would be more reliable than information that we'd obtained from an anonymous member of the public. The source grading ranges from 'always reliable' like telephone intercepts, to an 'untested source.' This latter grading refers to information that has been received from a first-time source. The information may not necessarily be unreliable, but it should be treated with caution and corroboration should be sought.

It is also essential that the actual information received from a source is evaluated for reliability. This will involve using an objective professional judgement, and the value of the information must not be exaggerated to encourage action to be taken. The assessment of the reliability of the information will be based on the person recording it and their knowledge of the circumstances at that time.

We apply a grading scale for the information that ranges from 'known to be true without reservation' to 'information that is suspected to be false.' This latter grading should be treated with extreme caution. It could be that the information has been supplied by malicious individuals. It has to be corroborated by a reliable source before any action is taken. Any person applying this grading must justify within the body of the report as to why it is appropriate to use this particular grading.

During these cases we get all manner of information coming into us. We need to apply the above grading systems so that we can decipher whether or not it's worth following up the source and putting in time and effort following intelligence leads and deploying our resources. Both of which can be in short supply.

I remember one way we'd obtained information in the past as being quite comical. Whilst it had always been a pleasure to work with the police officers and government agents stationed in Iraq, one guy who worked within the Hostage Affairs Department of the FBI and who had clearly watched too many Hollywood FBI movies and thought that his role should involve him acting like a character from one of these films.

It was at about eight in the evening on a cold night when I received a call from him, asking me to meet him in a little-known car park as he had some information to share with me. I decided to go along with it; after all, this could have been a real breakthrough in the case I was working on. What followed could have come straight out of a film, and a bad one at that. I waited in this dark, empty car park, shivering and wondering to myself if I was even in the right place. Then he appeared, creeping out of the shadows, wearing a long leather coat with a turned-up collar. I remember thinking from the onset that if that was my guy, he was clearly a total tosser. He approached me looking over his shoulder frequently, obviously wary of make-believe snipers. He handed me a small piece of folded up paper without saying a word, looking back over his shoulder and to his left and right surreptitiously as he did so. It was as if Jason Bourne were about to jump out and attack him, or maybe he thought *he* was Jason Bourne. I opened the piece of paper, only to find a closely penned Arabic name written across it.

I was becoming very impatient and tired of this crap 'What is this?' I asked with a dismissive tone. The guy just smiled, tapped the side of his nose in a secretive fashion and left. What the hell? Why couldn't he have said something? Anything? There I was left alone in this car park with a piece of paper delivered by a spy caricature. The next day I ran the name through our intelligence base, and guess what? Nothing. I was right, he was a tosser.

Our meetings in Iraq were held in various places, but our favourite by far was the (temporary) American Embassy that was used previous as Saddam Hussein's palace. We loved it there, a great place to meet our FBI colleagues, not least because it had a Starbucks in its main foyer and Ben and Jerry's ice cream in their canteen. Only in America. The palace was a mixture of ornate surroundings, gold plated doors, temporary wooden partitions, erected to make small offices out of such large rooms, and horses and missiles painted on the ceiling (courtesy of Saddam's commissioned artist). The Americans vacated this premises a couple of years after my last visit and now inhabit probably the largest embassy in the world. No surprise.

We had to be prepared for all manner of contact, from telephones, emails, newspaper adverts and walk in intermediaries.

Sometimes we managed to build good relations with the local law enforcement and Iraq is no different, although their manner of their working can be. The local police captain was a great guy always popping into the embassy for a chat and sharing what the word on the street was relating to our kidnapping. One day he was late for our usual meet and we couldn't raise him on his phone. We thought nothing of this until he turns up two hours late and claims he was in an armed ambush.

Slightly disbelieving his grand excuse for being late, we enquire as to what happened. 'come look at my car' he said. We walk out the main gate of the embassy and see his wreck of a Toyota which had several small, what looked like, bullet holes scattered down one side. 'Here look' he continues, as he walks and points at all the holes, opens the driver's door and points out small holes in the front and rear seats and the dashboard. 'Look this is where the bullets came in and just missed me!' Seems like I was wrong to doubt this brave man. 'So what happened?' I enquire. 'There were three of them, I shot two and they ran off, but I managed to get one and put him in the trunk and drive him to the station.' Now I would have doubted this story but seeing how the car was riddled with bullets and this man had been two hours late, I believed him. I also knew that the life expectancy for a cop in Iraq was short. Whenever someone is late for a meeting nowadays, any excuse pales into insignificance to this man's.

We always made sure we had a few phrases up our sleeve in case we were called on the phone by an Arabic speaker. I practised a few until I felt confident, often ringing my colleague Stephen to bounce the dialogue off him. They were statements such as, 'I don't speak Arabic, can you call back in ten minutes?' 'I will get an interpreter, please call back.' After one session of practice we were heading off to dinner when an excitable Intelligence Analyst ran over to us, asking that we join him urgently 'Upstairs. Now.'

The 'upstairs' is where the likes of MI5 and MI6 stealthily hung out and my god, were they an intense bunch. I was reprimanded once for ringing one of them on their mobile. They demanded to know why I rang their mobile number. 'I am not here in the country' they protested. 'obviously I am' they continued, 'but not known to others.' They are so far up their own arses.

Anyway, we dutifully followed this analyst like two excited lap dogs, passed the security doors and into the shadowy room. As we walked in a James Bond looking guy swivelled around to us in an office chair (seriously) and said 'We've had a breakthrough gentleman. We've been monitoring the telephones and have heard two guys with English accents speaking Arabic together.' I looked at Stephen and he looked sheepishly back at me. Obviously, we were the English guys that they'd overheard. In the end we had to tell the Sean Connery wannabe that it was us speaking and that his supposed 'breakthrough' was a load of pants. He looked embarrassed, gave us a short shrift and we were asked to leave the secret room that doesn't exist. By the man that isn't really there. But obviously is.

I've already mentioned the exciting journeys *into* Iraq earlier in this chapter but there was one particular journey *out* of Iraq that I recall with fondness.

We all crammed into the helicopter, about ten of us again, including some very important FCO chap. As we take off, I look back and see everyone suddenly leap under parked vehicles. How interesting I thought, this sudden desire to change engine oil. Maybe it was a 'who can tell me the make of the nearest exhaust pipe game?'

And then as soon as we take off, we suddenly land on a piece of waste ground about 30 seconds later. Unusual, because we normally fly for about twenty minutes to the airport. Do not stop, don't pass go, it's too dangerous etc., Still, I say nothing, firstly because no one would hear me over the rotors. Secondly, because no one will care about what I have to say. Thirdly, because I don't want to appear as though I don't know what is happening. Which, I don't. After about five minutes we take off again without having turned everything off or no one getting in or out. Interesting.

We continue to Baghdad Airport, land, and I check in as normal. It was about an hour later when Stephen arrives in the second run of helicopters. He runs up to me and shouts 'Fuck me, did you hear what happened?' 'Nope clearly not as I am not as excited as you at the moment, and if I had heard what you had heard I would probably be as demented as you.' 'Shut up wise ass' he replies. 'As you took off, three mortars came whizzing in and we had to duck for cover' (ah the diving under the cars I witnessed. 'Ah that's why we landed in a field!'

Isn't it nice how everyone keeps the dangerous things from you. It's a bit like when you are flying with BA and there is a major problem with the plane, they never tell you honestly what it is, in order to stop you panicking. They merely say something like 'ladies and gentlemen we have to take a slight change to our journey and return to Heathrow temporarily.' Which means, 'there's a really strange noise coming from engine number one and we think it might catch fire soon if we don't land quickly!' Another near miss taken for the FCO. The things you do to negotiate.

There were to be several more trips to this country to deal with more kidnappings of British citizens. More of the same journey shenanigans and more adventures. We did get to use the pool at times and I learned to pack my marmite in a more secure fashion. There were no more meetings in dark car parks, because I had learnt not to waste time with tossers. We also practiced Arabic without using the phones. The results of some of the cases were pretty shocking and we were not always successful in returning the hostages home. What I do know is everyone tried their hardest and we would not rest until all lines of enquiry had been exhausted. What I am proud of is that we did our very best and put as much time and resources into these cases as was humanly possible.

Baby snatch tactics

It's not all glamorous travel to far off desert lands, as the next few cases will show. In between these foreign jaunts I would remain on call and deal with the never-ending stream of incidents that occurred in London. This particular case unfolded during another cold and wet night when I received a phone call at 2 a.m. to assist in a negotiation to stop a man from killing his baby. I answered the phone bleary-eyed and yawning, only to be met with the following information. 'Martin, we have a man holding his baby hostage with a knife to its throat. He's volatile. He's threatening to kill the child if he isn't allowed custody.'

I dutifully fell out of bed, struggled to find my clothes in the half-darkness and dashed to my car. The incident was in Walthamstow, North London, about 15 miles away.

When I arrived at the scene some 30 minutes later, I was met by the coordinator superintendent, wearing a black woolly hat and a thick winter coat. He looked grimly unshaven, like a thug out of some low budget action thriller. He briefed me, with a touch of agitation in his voice.

'There is a man in a car,' he began. 'He has a baby in there with him, which is less than a year old. He is hungry and crying continuously.'

'The man or the baby?' I ask, breaking the tension.

The superintendent ignores me. 'He refuses to give the child back to the mother and has locked himself in the car. The car window is slightly open; you can talk to him through it. We have a doctor on site who has told us that the baby's health is not at risk. Good luck!'

Now at this time in my life I had two young children and knew well the sound of a baby in distress. It was an unbearable noise, a sound that tugs at your heartstrings. Perhaps reminding the father of the fact that his baby was suffering would be a good negotiating tactic to use in this scenario. Yet my carefully thought out strategy never seemed to take effect, as six hours into the negotiations later, we were still no closer to reaching a conclusion. The father flatly refused to get out of his car. He wanted nothing. We could offer him nothing. All he wanted was for us to go away. We briefly considered breaking the window and grabbing the baby, but good old dad still had the knife held close to the baby's throat and one false move would have been catastrophic. We kept talking, in an attempt to resolve what was now becoming a dangerous time for the baby's health.

The following gives you a fairly clear breakdown of the exchanges I made with dad.

M. So, what has brought you to do this today?

D. Fuck off.

M. You sound angry. We are here to help you and we are very worried about the baby.

D. So you should be, Fuck Face.

I am beginning to sense that this man had issues with authority.

Note my words *'you sound angry.'* As a Negotiator, you are taught to emotionally label a person's language and the non-verbal communication you observe. After all, we must always make an attempt to understand their position (however bonkers) to build rapport and establish a positive relationship. This is called emotional labelling. It allows us to express opinions in a non-judgemental way without causing offence whilst finding out what emotion the other person is feeling. We must learn to take responsibility for the language we use and the effect it is having on the person we're speaking to. We must avoid telling the other person how they feel. Instead we use phrases like *'you sound* frustrated with me,' *'I feel* as if you believe we have betrayed you' and even *'it seems* to me that you are upset with the situation.' These qualifying words result in either agreement or denial so that we're then able to get to the real emotions of the person. From there we can probe it with open questioning and draw ourselves nearer to reaching a conclusion.

M. Well, I am worried. I want the baby to remain safe and healthy.

H. It will if you allow me to drive off with him.

M. What's with the knife at his throat then?

H. If I can't have him, she can't.

M. She?

H. The bitch that called you.

M. Ah, would that be your wife?

H. Fuck off.

Anger is usually the first emotion we face when dealing with somebody in a crisis. It's understandable. It comes from a place of fear and the knowledge that they're in a situation they didn't anticipate being in.

M. Listen, you can hold your baby while you talk to me. But I am concerned about the knife. Can you stop holding it against his neck for me?

H. It stops you trying to get in the car.

M. We are not going to try and get in the car. It would be too dangerous for the baby for us to do that, as we would have to break the glass. My concern is the baby's safety, so we wouldn't do that.

H. Have you got kids?

M. I have two.

He's going to do the whole 'then you get where I'm coming from' bit.

D. (Sure enough) Then you get where I'm coming from. You know how much he means to me. She won't let me have access.

Really? I can't think why. You seem like such a calm, predictable sort of person, who really cares about your child.

M. Sounds awful for you. What have you done to ensure that you can have more time with your son?

H. Told her I should have him.

M. I see. Anything else? Have you discussed how it affects you and that it's good for the child for a father to have access?

H. Fuck off.

This is going marvellously.

It's difficult trying to deal with someone who doesn't listen. We are all bad listeners at times for numerous reasons. Here are a list of barriers to effective listening, things that we all do from time to time.

Passive listening /dreaming

You are half listening and something the other person says triggers a chain of associations of your own. You don't actually want to be there. You feel that what's being said to you is wasting your time and the time of the person talking to you.

Identifying

You refer everything the other person says to your own experience. You bring your own frame of reference and personality to what they are telling you. This leads to you asking questions so that it makes sense for you, rather than them.

Advising

You are the great problem-solver, ready with help and suggestions. You listen and then try and find a resolution that suits you. You start giving them advice on what they should or should not do, regardless of whether or not they've actually asked for your opinion.

Derailing

You suddenly change the subject. You derail the train of conversation when bored or uncomfortable, or you joke it off.

Placating

You want to be nice, pleasant, and supportive. You want people to like you. So you half listen, probably enough to get the drift, but without really absorbing what's being said.

Mind reading

You are trying to figure out what the other person is really thinking and feeling. You look for hidden meanings and do not trust or believe in what they are saying to you. This can include over-analysing body language.

Rehearsing

Your attention is on the preparation and delivery of your next comment. You are more interested in what you are going to say next rather than listening.

Judging

You have firm views, values and/or beliefs about what the other person is saying. You may not like the person. You have already made up your mind about what they are saying. You don't listen to what they say as you have already judged them. You look for words and sentences that support your own beliefs and focus on them rather than the whole conversation.

Think about which one of the above you do most. The next time you listen to what someone is telling you, make a conscious effort to take on a different strategy.

M. The baby sounds hungry. Why don't you allow us to feed it? If you step out of the car we can give you the milk and we won't grab you whilst you're feeding it.

D. Yeah right! I'm no mug. Why don't you pass the milk through the window?

M. I've been told that won't happen. You will have to step out for the milk.

D. Then you've got a long wait, because I'm sitting here until I get to talk to my wife here and have the milk in the car.

As discussed before, we don't like to bring the person they ask for to the scene. People in a crisis are usually more agitated which leads to arguments and this then hinders our own line of discussion.

M. What is it that makes you want her here?

D. To show her how serious I am.

M. I think she knows that from what you are doing.

Time for some persuasion skills

M. Look, you love your baby, right?

D. Of course.

M. So his safety is everything to you, right?

At this point, I'm trying to get him to latch on to a consistent thought about something. If someone openly agrees to a way they feel about something, it's more difficult for them not to continue to agree with that position when it is brought up in conversation at a later stage.

D. I don't think I need to answer that. Every dad is the same, man.

M. Good. But what you are now doing is contrary to those beliefs.

There we are! With this thought in mind, it should be difficult for him to continue to justify what he's doing.

D. Fuck off!

There are times in negotiating when we have to examine the possible reasons for why we're not reaching an agreement. It might be down to bad chemistry in that we haven't built up enough of a rapport with the person, so cannot begin to influence their behaviour. In some cultures, the fear of losing face holds a lot of sway. For example, a kidnapper who wants the government to make political concessions, which are being played out in full media glare, will need his ego fed and a good reason for ending the kidnap.

Another reason we reach an impasse might be because the person may not be ready for an agreement, either because they are not convinced by our argument or because they are not under enough pressure to reach one. Many kidnappers around the world have all the time they need to negotiate, as nobody is looking for the hostage they've taken. In the end, they give the hostage back, not because they feel they have been overcome, but because they've exhausted the victim's family of money and need to go out and find somebody else to kidnap. It's a business to them.

Some people won't give in because of an Inclination to resist perceived aggression. They feel that you are being aggressive by not giving them what they want, so resist any urge to comply. Finally, the kidnapper may feel like they are being misunderstood or mistreated, which makes them angry and inflexible when it comes to negotiating.

M. Listen, I'm just trying to save this baby. I am worried you will harm him, OK? Why not give him back today and then we can put you in touch with a good solicitor who can talk to you about custody rights. If you have been unfairly treated, you may have a good case.

D. I *do* have a case.

M. There you are then.

We seem to have reached a turning point in the negotiations. He hasn't told me to fuck off and he appears to be listening to what I'm saying. We call this 'progress.' Well done, Martin-

D. Fuck off!

Right.

M. Is it your weekend to have the child, then?

D. Every weekend should be mine. It's my fucking child and she's a bitch.

M Who, your wife?

D. She can't cook. She's shit in bed. She's a crap mum and she's fat.

So why did you marry her then, you slim, attractive Michelin-chef, stud of the year?

M. You must have loved her at some point?

D. Lusted after her more like.

M. I see. Your son there, I'm sure you love him and want him to be fed now?

D. Bring the milk and I'll feed him.

M. We have talked about this, remember?

I was just about to continue our conversation when suddenly, out of nowhere, I saw the father open the car door, the baby still in his arms, and the knife still at his throat. I saw him step out on to the pavement, with total nonchalance. He began to walk off down the road as if he were on his way to take his baby to the park. He was headed towards the police cordon at the end of the road, set up to prevent members of the public from interfering in our operation. I rolled my eyes at this utterly thoughtless behaviour and immediately decided to follow him, negotiating as I went.

M. Listen, it's great that you are out of the car, but walking around the streets with a weapon at a baby's throat is really not a good move. The officers have placed a cordon at the end of the street and I strongly suggest you don't walk beyond it.

D. You forced me to do this.

M. Where are you thinking of walking to?

H. Wherever I feel like.

M. You are going to force someone's hand soon. You can't walk around the streets holding a knife when there are other people about. That's why we sealed off the street in the first place. We can't afford to bring other people into contact with you if you are upset and have a weapon. We have a responsibility to the public.

H. Well I am going walk right through your so-called cordon anyway.

M. Not recommended. I ask you to please remain in this street and discuss getting milk to your son.

H. Just watch me.

M. I'd rather you stood still and thought about this.

(Whilst my earlier negotiation was going on, I was completely unaware of the fact that 12 officers from our tactical public order branch were standing around the corner, out of view, one hundred yards behind me. They were practicing 'how to take a baby out of the arms of an irate father' tactic with a small plastic doll they'd somehow managed to obtain. I have no idea how (perhaps one officer had brought it to work with him, lest the situation to rescue a baby had ever come into fruition). Yet there they were, continuing the practice of this Bruce Lee-like manoeuvre whilst I was previously standing by the car door talking to this father about milk and custody rights).

I continued walking alongside him, striding towards the ever-approaching cordon. I knew there would be a confrontation if he decided to push past the officers, which had the potential to injure the baby, the officers and even Mr Obnoxious. I decided to move forwards and stand stationary in front of him – he would have to physically push me out of the way then – but it didn't help. He merely ran around me and made a break for the cordon tape.

Just as I was considering tackling him to the ground, in charged the baby squad team and – snatch! Twelve men went in, twelve men and a baby came out, with the suspect restrained and no physical damage to anyone. I'd never seen anything like it! Apparently, they each had a role to play, a limb and a body part to take hold of and had tried several different methods using this very basic principle which had, marvellously, paid off. Safely in the hands of the police officers, the baby promptly stopped crying. Dad was taken in to custody and later charged with the attempt to abduct. And once again, the wisdom of negotiation strategy had played an important role in bringing us to victory. Sort of.

Dog Day Afternoon in Starbucks

Now onto some stories about armed sieges. In this chapter I will share for you a few armed tactics and deployment considerations, along with some negotiation strategies. Dog Day Afternoon, being the title of this chapter, refers back to my training course and the video we watched on arrival. This siege was situated in a Starbucks in Kensington, London. I remember finding this irritating as I prefer Costa coffee and if I'm going to be holed up at a siege for hours on end, at the very least I'd like access to well roasted coffee beans. I was in charge of the negotiations that day as 'on call' coordinator. On my arrival, I noticed that the local police had set up an incident room in a bar specifically for our purpose. The ground floor was a hive of activity. Armed response officers were running around in the usual body armour, puffing out their chests and generally looking macho.

The Borough chief inspector was briefing his staff, saying things like 'cordon', 'containment' and 'prisoner transport.' There were flip charts, makeshift tea stations and marker pens being thrown around as people made plans. At this point, my negotiator had arrived and we sit down for a briefing from the officer in charge.

'We have a man armed with a handgun. He went in to rob Starbucks, but as he was leaving a member of the public saw him acting suspiciously and alerted a passing uniformed sergeant. The sergeant approached the Starbucks just as the suspect was attempting to leave with his loot. Rather than shoot the Sergeant, he panicked, rounded up the staff and ushered them into the basement. The premises were contained quickly so we know he is still in there.' He finished this last sentence with a sigh, his moment of 'briefing glory' now over for the day.

From our perspective, this was an easy crime to handle. A crime had gone wrong. Staff were trapped in a venue. I set about briefing my negotiator with a strategy. We explored what our method of communication would be and where would be best to position ourselves.

There were several options. We could do a limited entry with the firearms team, gain access to the top of the stairs, crouch behind some ballistic shields and shout down into the basement. Or, we could remain outside, breach the main door and again, shout into the premises. Or, we could try and obtain the mobile telephone number of the kidnapper and talk properly. The last option however would prove problematic, as the basement would undoubtedly have poor phone signal. A perfect solution would be to get what we call a 'field phone' into the premises and talk via that. It's a dedicated phone, usually fed in with a wire and ensures that the kidnapper will talk only to us, which in turn opens up intelligence opportunities. It's always best to talk on a phone in these situations, rather than shouting from the outside. It makes it easier to build rapport and also means that members of the public can't nosey in on the conversations we're having.

When talking on a telephone we have to use what we term *minimal encouragers.* Minimal encouragers are phrases such as 'and?', 'really?', 'then?', 'uh huh', 'go on', 'odd', 'great', and 'interesting.' They're important phrases to use during telephone calls because kidnappers and the like need to know that you're listening. If the offending party has been speaking for an extended period of time and then ends up saying 'Are you still there?' it means we, the negotiator, haven't been using enough minimal encouragers. It's also important to match the pace of the encouragers with the kidnappers' speed of talking and you can change the pace of the encouragers to suit your preference.

As we were discussing our plan of attack, an unattended mobile phone at the table next to me began vibrating. I could hear it ringing and see it bouncing across the table, but no one was answering it. I'm not sure why this annoyed me, or why I thought this call might be important, but I was drawn to it. It was instinctive, which is something one must always hold in regard when it comes to this kind of work. Intuition works by matching patterns. In the same way that an experienced pilot looks at a wealth of instruments and immediately knows if something is not quite right, intuition matches what you are seeing with your own wealth of personal knowledge and experience. For this reason, we are usually more at risk in unfamiliar territory as our instinct is likely to mis-fire. Often, if we cannot find a logical reason for what our intuition is telling us, we disregard it. It's worth remembering that intuition has more strength than the logical mind. It is much faster and has access to our store of experience and training. It can pick up on danger through subtle cues, be it a car in the wrong place or behaviour that is incongruous, long before the conscious mind can. I *knew* this phone was important. Suddenly, without warning, a man who looked quite important walked over to the phone, picked it up, spoke into the phone and then threw it at me.

'It's for you' he said with nonchalance.

Really? I thought. When I'm in a place where no one knows me, where no one I know is aware I am there and an unattended mobile phone rings and someone I don't know, who doesn't own the phone, answers it, and throws it at me, and says 'it's for you', *it comes as some surprise!*

I take the phone and say 'Hello' and hear a whisper at the other end of the line. 'Hello, we are in a storeroom and he is outside pacing up and down with a gun. What's going on and what shall we do?'

Thee chance of this being another siege in another Starbucks around Kensington was quite small and so I presumed that the caller was a hostage from our incident. It was now my turn to play the 'I'm going to throw the mobile phone at someone', game. I threw the phone at my negotiator (this was becoming a grown-up version of pass the parcel) and mouthed the words 'hostage.' He nodded and went into autopilot giving the correct advice whilst in intelligence gathering mode.

It's important to communicate the correct advice to hostages. This advice should be practical, reassuring and should help to keep them safe. We tell them not to do anything to antagonise their kidnapper and that we are doing everything we can to get them home safe. We talk about the future, that we are looking forward to seeing them when they come out. We always assume that the kidnapper is listening, so we are very careful about trying to gather evidence. The hostage may be forced to say things they don't want to. He may be telling lies in order to put us under pressure.

Hostages who have been in captivity for some time should be given advice that helps them maintain their basic needs. This will ensure they will be less stressed while being detained, and hopefully recover quicker post release.

Advice includes:

Maintain their fitness and sleep discipline. Eat whenever possible, asking for medication if needed. Aim to calm situations and avoid questioning their kidnappers. Set tasks and goals to allow the hostage to focus on the 'now' rather than their unpredictable future. Maintaining a daily schedule is key to this. Build relationships and rapport where possible. Use memories to create connections with family and friends.
Commit to self-respect and behaviour that is necessary for survival, whilst having confidence in their ability to survive and in the actions of those back home. Take pride in being flexible and adaptable whilst maintaining some decision-making power, however small, and finally, engaging in humour, which releases tensions and provides a form of resistance.

At this point I had to establish whose phone we were speaking through. How did the hostage come by this number? Why was it unattended? Why did the hostage ring that particular phone? I approached several officers and the local inspector and investigated accordingly. It turned out to be an armed response officers' phone. He had been talking to a hostage prior to my arrival and had left his phone unattended when he went to the loo. Super professional, I thought. He hadn't even briefed us on the content of the earlier calls he'd made, or how many people he'd spoken to, or the mood of the hostages, or any intelligence he'd gained from speaking to them. In fact, he hadn't told us naff all!

The negotiator came back to me after five minutes of speaking to the hostage. During that time I watched with interest as armed response teams prepped plans in case they had to enter. I looked to my right where the chief inspector was running around, ordering the moving of cordons and briefing his boss who happened to be the important looking man who had initially picked up the mobile and thrown it at me. He was telling his officers about the local community's concerns. The public were worried that they couldn't get their usual double espresso from Starbucks and were asking if this would be a regular event. If it were to be, then they would go to Costa to get their beverages in the future. (These were genuine first world problems and concerns from the West London community, which I planned to address as soon as the innocent people in the Starbucks basement were released).

The following conversation has a few participants, so I've included a cast list for clarity on who's speaking.

M. Me.

N. Stephen (Negotiator).

I. Firearms Inspector.

S. Suspect.

H. Hostage.

N. Governor?

M. What have you got?

N. Well the hostage tells me there are about six staff, all of them are in the storeroom. He's locked them in and he is pacing around with a gun.

Trapped criminals often act liked caged animals. They want to escape and they're being contained, unexpectedly, against their will so they start to pace.

M. OK. We will try to get some communication with the kidnapper and work out if it's feasible to reach the main door. If it is, we can talk at the entrance from the street first with a view to moving to the top of the stairs inside later, if we need to.

N. Cool!

M. Cool? What are you 15?

N. Sorry Guv, it's my first shout. It's exciting!

Ah, 'the first call out' buzz. By this point, I was about eight years into my role and becoming quite cynical of all these people threatening to kill themselves and others. (as you may have gathered whilst reading this book).

That said, this was quite a sexy call out. I mean there were guns around, body armour, big six battery torches and smoke bombs.

M. Right, well, let's talk about strategy.

N. OK.

M. You start then. What do we think?

N Erm... well, he knows he isn't going anywhere. He knows he's getting arrested, so he's desperate. We need to give him some reassurance and a reality check.

M. Agreed. He probably thinks the armed lot are going to burst in and take him out. We need to get an idea of what their plans are, so we don't deliberately lie to him,

N. Roger that!

M. Whatever.

Roger that? Jesus, he must be ex-military.

I see him walk over to talk to the Firearms Commander. I know exactly what he's going through. I used to perform that role some years earlier, as a Firearms Team Leader in the Metropolitan Police. Right now, he'll be ensuring that the containment is in place and sending his sergeant around the building perimeter to check what his officers can see of the premises and suspect. We always need to know of the visual limitations in case the officers are called upon to fire. After a quick chat with the commander, he returns to me.

N. Right. The firearms guys want to breach the door to give us talking capability. We can't find a mobile number for the kidnapper and we might not get a signal, so this seems like a sensible idea.

M. I think we should keep trying. Do we know who he is? Can we do a network subscriber check to see if he has a phone registered to him?

N. No, we don't know who he is.

M. Then I think we should engage with the hostage that has the phone. Maybe he can give us some more intelligence if he's out of earshot from the guy.

I think this is a perfect scenario to detail for you, the reader, what decision making a firearms commander has to go through before deploying his officers and involving the use of firearms.

Firstly, they will examine all the *information and intelligence* to establish the following:

- Who the victim is, what the location is, what's the subject of intelligence
- What is known now?
- What could be known?
- What should be known?
- What information is available – is It FACT or an ASSUMPTION?
- What further enquiries can be made?
- Has the intelligence been graded or verified?
- What additional investigation can be carried out?
- Would they want to see any informant and how would they test the intelligence?
- How do they become intrusive?
- Who personally would they speak to, in order to check on the intelligence? How far down the chain is that person?

They would then carry out a *threat assessment.*

- Is there a known or unknown threat?
- What is the associated threat in the scenario?
- How has the threat been assessed and graded?
- How has this assessment been recorded?

- Where is the greatest area of threat and when will it be?
- Who is under threat now?
- Who could potentially be under threat?
- Do resources need to be deployed immediately to mitigate the identified threat?
- Are initial control measures required?
- Are they increasing the intelligence/information whilst containing the threat?

They would then set a *strategy* with the following considerations.

- What's the priority order?
- How and when will they review it?
- What's their role?
- What are the tactical parameters?
- How does this strategy sit with the priorities set in the investigative strategy?
- Should the investigate strategy be included in the overall strategy?
- How will any conflicts be resolved and who will arbitrate in these circumstances?
- Are they going to attend the briefing?

It's important then to examine what *powers and internal policy* they have to deal with in the incident. They must consider the following:

- What legal powers need to be considered?
- Has an offence been committed?
- Is the strategy/tactical intention proportionate/lawful?
- Are the actions in line with any Manuals of Guidance or policy?
- Is the information/intelligence and associated threat sufficient to justify issuing firearms?

Once the previous questions have been examined and firearms are considered necessary, the **tactical options** will be identified.

Strategic Commanders need to understand tactical options to assist with setting parameters and constraints. They need to know how they would measure the effectiveness of each option to be able to identify the most appropriate one. For example, we need to test out tactics against our strategy, whether they mitigate the threats posed and adhere to the right to life principle of the European Convention on Human Rights (ECHR).

The tactical decisions of when to arrest and enter buildings is a command decision, out of the hands of the negotiator coordinator. The decision is always made by the tactical commander on the ground, in this case the chief inspector.

Firearms teams have several options.

Containment and Call Out. This is a tactic consisting of an inner-armed containment around a building, usually supported by an outer (usually) unarmed cordon.

Contact is initiated and the occupants of the address are called out and secured. The control of the person is then passed to an unarmed 'arrest' team, often parked up nearby in a police van that is briefed and ready to receive. The method of contact will vary from telephones, loud hailers or limited entry into the building.

Once all identified persons are under police control, the firearms team will conduct a slow 'search to contact,' to ensure that no further armed threats exist and that no more suspects are in hiding. This will usually involve the use of a police dog.

On completion of this slow search, the scene handover will take place between the firearms team leader and the scene commander.

In many forces, the containment and call-out tactic is accompanied by a *limited entry*. The necessity of this should be considered for each operation, but the advantages are such that:

- (i) It enables the rapid deployment of other tactics such as entry to save life, specialist munitions and less lethal options

- (ii) It provides a tactical advantage to the firearms team, which includes vision into the premises, greater control of movement inside and clear verbal control.

The use of this *limited entry* tactic must be considered against the threat assessment, strategy and ECHR responsibilities. It might not be appropriate in the event of there being vulnerabilities associated with the occupants or premises.

Dynamic Intervention. Sometimes it might be necessary to initiate this option on the basis that it is more likely to prevent death or serious injury arising from unlawful violence that way.

There are two types of *dynamic interventions*, one being to respond to a rapidly innovated and initiated option with a less than likely chance of success. This strategy is implemented only when the situation is dire and when extreme danger towards members of the public, the hostage or the police is obvious. It is a simple plan rapidly innovated and initiated to save the lives of the hostages.

The other is a concise, practised and detailed plan which is initiated only after a protracted incident takes place and where, in the view of the Gold/Silver Commander, (those in charge of the whole incident) will be lost unless a rescue plan is invoked immediately.

So now you are all experts in firearms tactics, let's get back to our incident. We're going to speak to the hostage remember?

N. So, I will call him back, then?

M. Yes and be careful when evidence gathering in case the kidnapper is listening. Just give him advice and reassure him and see what he says.

I hand my Negotiator a check-list.

Remember, when talking to a hostage, one must assume that the kidnappers can hear the conversation. We must use active listening skills at all times and avoid interruptions. It's important to acknowledge the hostage's fears and worries about the situation.

N. Hello

H. Hello

(*Whispering*)

N. So, um, we are doing all we can to get you out.

H. Like what?

(*Silence*)

H. Hello?

N. We are doing lots, but we want to talk to the person that's got you trapped in there.

H. I can't get to him. He's locked us in the storeroom and he is outside with a gun.

N. Can you get his attention?

H. OK, I will bang on the door.

N. Good man.

At this stage I'm thinking a tall latte would be nice, but now is probably not the right time to order one off a trapped barista. We hear banging. There's no response.

H. He's ignoring me.

N. OK.

H. My battery is going-

N. OK hang up.

(*Click*).

M. Right, we can either wait until he makes contact or breach the door and talk from upstairs. So, two options really.

N. Right.

M. So?

N. Right.

M. No, please don't have any ideas. I will have them all!

N. Right.

I approach the firearms team leader. As I say, I used to be a firearms leader many years ago, I know how they work and the type of personality they have. (Stereotyping I know).

Whilst in that role I used to hate negotiators turning up at a siege. We would be there ready to arrest someone and then some commander would call out the negotiators. Before we knew it, we were stuck outside Number 3 Granby Terrace for seven hours on the trot, whilst some *smooth-talking pill in a suit* tried to convince the kidnapper that he'd be better off giving himself up. I used to think like that, I really did. But then I became one of them and crossed over to the dark side.

M. Hello Inspector.

I. Yo.

Another fifteen-year-old teenager?

M. Yo, so we would like to talk to this man. Can you get us in and a bit closer?

I. Yo, no worries, just briefing the troops.

Of course you are. You live in your Iraq 2003 invasion world. Go ahead. Brief your troops, Captain America!

He walked off and approached a group of body armour wearing officers who were clicking the safety catches of their MP5 machine guns on and off, whilst lovingly stroking their Glock 17 pistol grips. (like I say I used to be one of them, so I can have a little dig).

I. (The Inspector briefs his men) Right men, the negs want to speak to this guy face to face, or at the very least within earshot. But we haven't got a phone for him and he's refusing to talk to us. So, we're going to breach the door, take them to the entrance and hold for them to negotiate behind our shields.

He then looks at me.

I. Yo, you need to put on your body armour and stay behind the shields. OK?

M. Of course.

We don our body armour and exit the pub, walking slowly behind the armed team as they walk towards Starbucks, which has been locked by the kidnapper. The scene must look bizarre. Six armed personnel walking gingerly behind ballistic shields in a crab like fashion, their side arms drawn. Immediately behind them, over their shoulders, are a couple more guys pointing longer barrelled MP5 machine guns forward. And finally, behind them stands myself and my negotiator. All my concentration is going into trying to remain upright and not tripping up into the armed officer in front. Imagine if he tripped over thanks to my feet and ended up shooting the ankle of the colleague next to him!

We approach the premises. One officer takes out a crow bar and prises open the metal frame that surrounds the main entrance glass door. This pops it open. At this point I'm concerned by the noise we're creating. If the kidnapper hears us, he might get hysterical and begin thinking that we're here to take him out. I need my negotiator to say quickly that we are not here to harm him, but merely to talk from upstairs at the door and that we will not enter the premises. My negotiator begins shouting into the premises.

N. Hello, its Stephen I'm with the police and we want to help solve this safely. Can you hear me?

(Silence)

N. Listen, no one is coming down to get you provided you look after the people you have down there.

(Silence)

N. What's your name? I know you don't want to be trapped in there and things haven't turned out the way you wanted today but-

S. I ain't going inside, OK?

(The voice shouts from the basement area and we notice a set of stairs that lead down from the rear of the building).

N. I can't say what's going to happen. Let's take this one step at a time, OK?

S. I have a gun and I will use it!

N. Now at this moment no one has been hurt, which is good news and means you will be treated more favourably when this ends. We will ensure that you get good legal advice, as is your right. There is no need for you to harm anyone. How are the people down there with you?

Bloody hell, my colleague's doing well. And here we are, sweating our socks off in safety gear, on our knees behind ballistic shields. In all honesty, I shouldn't be here with my negotiator right now. My role as a coordinator is to be with the other strategic and tactical leaders back at the pub. But I took a decision to stay with him to give him support until the next negotiator arrives. It's not ideal, but hey. I'm flexible.

S. Look, I could have shot that sergeant who stopped me leaving the place, but I didn't.

N. I know, so-

S. (Shouting louder now) And I have looked after this lot down here, so show me some fucking respect!

Oh dear, another ego that needs feeding. These kidnappers are such high maintenance. It's Stephen's turn to show some empathy and build some rapport.

It's important to remember the distinction between demonstrating sympathy and showing empathy. Empathy is where you come to grips with a problem, as the person is informing you of the reality as they perceive it. We must deal with the kidnappers' realities.

Empathy is not about being nice and it is not the same as sympathy. Sympathy is an expression of pity, sorrow, distress for another. Empathy is the identification of another's situation and motive. Making the attempt to get it right is important as it creates a positive atmosphere for problem solving. Understanding is *not* agreeing and it's important to refrain from arguing and to listen without judgement, whilst acknowledging the kidnapper's point.

N. Well, thank you for looking after those people. It's good that you are keeping them from harm and we are grateful for this. Would you at least think about letting them go?

This is another good thing to say because we all like to appear to others to be consistent in our thinking and behaviour. If someone publicly announces a core value, attitude, intended action or belief, it's harder for them to back out of these declarations if asked later. (Restaurant staff asked callers, who were booking a table, to call back if they change their minds and couldn't attend. This simple act of obtaining this commitment reduced the amount of unannounced no shows). If a kidnapper commits publicly to an action, they will be more likely to carry it out. If our suspect agrees to look after our hostage that's good news and goes some way in the safe release being achieved

S. Yeah, I will think about letting them go.

(A moment passes).

S. There. Thought about it. And no, I won't.

Oh, you're so funny, you arrogant, cocky gun wielding git.

N. Now these people have done nothing wrong. They have been caught up in something that even you didn't plan. I think you wanted to come in here and steal money, but because you couldn't leave, you are now in a situation that I don't think you wanted. So, let's talk about how we can get everyone out of there safely and make sure that you are dealt with fairly. What do you say?

Not bad at all. In fact, very good.

S. True enough. So how are we going to solve this, detective?

He's not a detective, you idiot, he's a negotiator.

N. I think a start would be letting these poor, scared people go.

S. And then?

Good question. I'd ask the same.

N. And then you come out safely and we give you some legal rep and you say this was never your intention, that you just panicked-

S. I never panic!

I somehow knew he would say that.

N. Alright, then you acted out of desperation.

S. I'm never desperate!

For heaven's sake man, admit something.

N. OK, then you can say that you were forced into a situation you never intended.

S. OK that sounds better.

Yes, I bet it does.

Kidnappers can have the following characteristics:

- They're driven by ego.
- They show little to no remorse.
- They are destructive.
- They are not insane but know right from wrong and choose not to conform to right.
- They enjoy controlling others.
- They have low tolerance for frustration.
- They have a need to prove that they can do something worthwhile.

We can address these characteristics by:

- Expecting demands.
- Keeping their ego in mind (they need to feel in charge).
- Adopting a real-world approach to negotiation.
- Being aware of false promises.

- Helping them save face or by convincing them that they're not failures.

- Talking of success and raising their self-esteem.

- Convincing them that the safe release of a victim works to their advantage.

- Praising their ability to make tough and realistic decisions.

Back to Starbucks.

S. Here's the deal.

N. OK.

S. I want a guarantee of no prison, and a good solicitor, and for the guns you got up there to back off because I don't trust them cunts. I watch the news; they can be a bit trigger happy if you know what I mean.

I want, I want, I want. Me, me, me. I think we need to manage his expectations. I think he needs to be realistic, and obviously, I think he needs a slap.

N. Now we can get you a solicitor. But we can't pull away the armed guys because we have been told that you have a firearm. They are here to protect the public, not to harm you. We have a duty to protect people and that's the only reason they are here. I can assure you that if you come up the stairs with no weapon, they won't shoot you because you pose no threat to them. And I will be here with them to witness their actions. I haven't lied to you and I don't intend on doing so.

S. I ain't going back to prison.

N. Like I say, no one knows what is going to happen afterwards. But you haven't harmed anyone so that's good news in your favour.

S. Whatever.

This is often a sticking point with trapped criminals. They have a fear of imprisonment. When their fear of going to jail crops up however, I'm always tempted to ask them why they didn't hold that factor in consideration before robbing a premises with a gun and taking a load of people hostage.

But we need to give him hope and a reason to surrender. We like not to lie, but we do like to project a 'glass half full' attitude. Even though it may be bollocks

N. So how do you see today ending?

S. I have to think. I ain't going to prison. There might be another way out.

N. Like?

Silence. Sometimes it's good to allow people space to think. 'Effective Silence' we call it.

N. Hello?

S. Shut the fuck up! You are going to have to guess.

Oooh a quiz! Let's guess away. A) He is going to build a tunnel and escape from the basement. B) He is going to dress up in a Starbucks apron, pretend to be a hostage and smuggle himself out. C) He is hoping we'd just get bored and go away.

N. Now the safest way to solve this is for you to walk up the stairs to us. We can walk you across the road where we will have a solicitor waiting for you. And from there, we can talk about some options.

S. Yeah and then we can talk about how many years I'll probably get.

Time for a reality check

N. Well without knowing your past record, it's hard to say. What is fair to say though is that you have taken hostages with a gun and committed an armed robbery. You are trapped here with armed officers. If you injure people you will go to prison for longer than if you let people go. We know you are in control down there, but you have the power to end this safely. We are in your hands.

Is that smoke I can smell? Is that…he's started a fire!

'Go, go, go!' a shout rings out and penetrates my left ear. Eh? I'm temporarily dazed and confused. Suddenly, ten armed officers run quite literally over my head, throw me to the floor and leg it down the stairs to rescue the hostages. I hear shouts of 'armed police' and 'show me your hands!'

Whatever, I think. They love it. I lie on the deck with Stephen and think, this negotiating lark isn't all it's cracked up to be. We either bore people into submission, or they're so desperate for the toilet, they come off that roof they are on, or they fall asleep. In this case they start a fire, which means the negotiating ends and the uniform police have to step in to save lives. This incident reminded of Batman who was rushed by the rope team.

I hear more voices and, before long, hysterical crying. I can't tell if it's the kidnapper or the hostages bawling his eyes out over the situation. I then see the hostages being pushed up the stairs towards me, still dressed in their green overalls with their name badges still on. They pass me, one by one. Edgar, Zach, Joanne. Five people in all, each one a more ominous shade of shell-shocked white than the last.

As this was a sudden deployment, the arrest team and hostage reception committee were not yet in position. So, we hand them over to some unarmed cops on the outer containment, who guide them across into the pub opposite in order to get them away from the venue and kidnapper. I waited to see the kidnapper walking up the stairs in handcuffs before making my exit.

You often get a picture of what a person looks like when talking to them on the phone, but this man looked nothing like I imagined. I thought he would be a Reggie Kray, 1960's gangster lookalike. Instead he looked more like Woody Allen, which was disappointing for me and probably him. (No offence Woody).

He was eventually processed and charged with a serious offence. The fire was started by setting alight cardboard in a bin in the basement. I don't think he would have burnt the place down. I believe it was his way of saving face by prompting an armed intervention rather than having to surrender. (Sounds better for him when he is recounting his story to his prison mates). All the hostages were offered some form of counselling and no doubt shared all their experiences on social media. Starbucks probably reviewed their security policies and ensured all premises were as secure as they could be, and staff training was enhanced. All that said, you will never stop an armed suspect intent on committing a crime in a public coffee shop. So, until the next time.

Britain's longest siege

The Hackney Siege, or 'Britain's Longest Siege' for want of a better title, was brought to my attention on Boxing Day, 26th of December 2002, much to the annoyance of my children and mother in law. It was an extremely cold winter period if I recall and I had arrived at the scene with flashing blue lights only to be told that an armed suspect who had shot at armed police was contained inside a flat. Blimey, I'd thought, this isn't the type of call you get every day.

Here is an extract from a newspaper article which summarises the incident two years after it took place.

An armed suspect at the centre of one of Britain's longest sieges escaped death when a police bullet went through his mouth, only for him to shoot himself in the head, a coroner ruled.

Eli Hall, 29, who had a string of convictions for violence, drug and firearms offences, spent 15 days holed up in a bedsit in Hackney, in East London, from December 26th 2002, before setting the building alight and killing himself on January 9th 2003.

Paul OKere, 22, a student who lived in the same building, told the inquest at St Pancras Coroner's court how he had escaped to safety five days earlier, after being held hostage by Hall for eleven days.

Paul had said that he had woken late on Boxing Day to find the front door barricaded and the place surrounded by police. During his time as a hostage, Paul had tried to reason with Eli. The two men had even cooked meals togethe,r but Mr. OKere had become increasingly terrified and had eventually managed to escape when Hall was upstairs.

The siege, which sparked a £1m Scotland Yard operation, started on Boxing Day when police sent a civilian contractor to take away Hall's car for forensic examination in connection with other crimes.

Armed officers were nearby in case Hall, who had shot at police on two occasions in 2002, returned to the car. But they had no idea the vehicle was parked outside his home in Hackney.

Hall opened a window and threatened the contractor, who ran off. Hall then shot at armed officers as they tried to get him to come outside.

Police stated they were in constant contact with Hall in the days that followed, urging him to give himself up. But Hall, who fired on police several times throughout the siege, insisted he was not going back to jail.

'The man in the street with a gun will always be top dog,' he told police. 'Bring it on. This is war.'

Negotiators had talked to Hall by mobile phone for hours, assuring him police would not harm him if he gave himself up. He had asked for a written guarantee that he would not go to jail, which police were unable to provide.

The suspect fired on police and they fired back what turned out to be the shot which went through Hall's mouth. Then smoke was seen billowing from the windows and police fought to get the blaze under control.

When armed officers later got into the building, they found Hall's charred body in the hallway. He had a handgun on his chest, and four other guns, ammunition, and gun-making equipment were discovered in the house.

So that's the official story. I will now explain how my colleague and I were the first two people to speak to Eli and Paul and also moments during the siege.

In those days after receiving a call I'd usually get collected at the M1 motorway services en route to London. This is to ensure that I could get to the scene as fast as possible. This was called a 'fast run' and was always authorised by the chief Inspector in charge of emergency calls for the Met. I would telephone the number after being asked to attend. I would supply my name and rank and the incident number. There were traffic department 'fast run' drivers in charge of these pick-ups and they were hilarious motor geek stereotypes. They'd spend every journey discussing (in detail) car lanes, car speed, whether they could pass on the left or right hand side of the car in front, whether there were some excellent overtakes (yawn) all the while driving through the London traffic at an alarming speed that would make you grit your teeth and wish you'd never got in the car to begin with.

They never failed to praise each other on their driving ability and we always managed to arrive intact (no doubt with the brakes red hot and glowing). These traffic division officers took their driving extremely seriously, so much so that I once heard of a traffic cop who liked to light a cigarette after a fast run on his brake discs. Can anyone be that sad? It turns out, if they're from traffic division, they can be.

I arrived at the call and set about trying to find the person in charge. I wanted to ask all the usual questions: what did we already know about the suspect? What had triggered the incident? Who was currently talking to him? Any and all information at that stage that was crucial.

As I was trying to find someone that was in charge, I immediately heard the sound of gun shots. I quickly headed towards the allocated 'rendezvous point' (RVP) and found a uniformed sergeant. He informed me that the inspector was taking cover behind a building nearby and that the armed response crew was negotiating with the criminal from a police vehicle via a mobile phone.

I remember glancing around and getting a lay of the environment. We were in a residential area, with blocks of flats and narrow streets surrounding us on either side. It was the day after Christmas and every one of those residential flats was no doubt full up with families, curled on the sofa watching mindless television programmes. This residential area had the potential for voyeurs (and indeed press attention) even more likely. Before long we'd have hundreds of residents craning out of their living room windows, camera phones at the ready in order to get a peek of the action during the Queens's Christmas address to the nation.

I established where the vehicle containing the armed officers was located and decided it was safe to approach them. I knocked on the steamed-up windows, identified myself and sat down in the back with another negotiator who'd also just arrived. The front passenger was on the phone to the suspect and it was apparent that he was doing his level best to calm down or suspect, or should I say persuade him to 'come out and give himself up.' There are certain words that we try to avoid using when dealing with these type of incidents. 'Calm down' is two of them as, in general, it's always better to soften the language and make it less emotive. For example, rather than using the word *hostage,* we use the first name of the person we're referring to. Rather than the word *demand*, it's better to say, 'what you have asked for.' *Kidnap* becomes 'people taken against their will who are being held.' *Deadline* becomes 'the time frame you have set us.'

I listen carefully as the officer deals with the suspect. When the call ends, he lets out a sigh and turns to face us with a serious expression.

'What have we got?' I ask.

'He tried to shoot at us when we attempted to gain entry. We retreated here, and he told us that if we got any closer he'd fire again. So far communication is strictly through mobile.'

I could see that this officer was finding the situation incredibly difficult. Beads of sweat were glistening on his forehead and his ashen white face made him resemble a hospital patient. Poor guy. Prior to my arrival, he would have probably had zero training on how to approach negotiation. At a pinch he might have had some verbal advice from the negotiating coordinator on how to proceed until back up arrived.

General advice for police officers who are non-negotiators and who arrive first on scene includes:

- Have someone with you to coach if possible.

- Make all calls in a silent area.

- Always have a pen and paper to hand.

- Plan for 'what if's'

- Write down what you want to know, your objectives for the call and any number that displays on your phone.

- Be prepared for threats/ violence/ distressed people.

- Explain that you are willing to listen.

- Introduce delay (gain time to gather funds, gain intelligence, resource the incident, establish and prepare for the motive).

- Use the hostage name and refer to the hostage family and loved ones (so as to personalise the hostage).

- Avoid official language, jargon (e.g. Proof of life).

- Ask after the wellbeing and health of hostage; seek evidence that they are alive. Ask if we can speak with the hostage, persuade the offender that if hostage is well and they can prove this then the victim/company/family is more likely to engage positively.

- Agree a number, time and code word for the next call so as not to miss the call and to reassure yourself that you know who you are dealing with.

- Advise the offender that you are the sole person to speak to for the purpose of resolving the negotiation. Persuade the offender that it is more beneficial for them to communicate with one person for continuity and to avoid confusion.

- Encourage them to believe in you.
- Gain rapport and trust to establish influence. (Guard against becoming too familiar).
- Give thanks for kindness and apologise for mistakes and misunderstandings. Say sorry if appropriate.
- Avoid inviting demands and deadlines. Comments like, 'I need two hours, how long do I have?' should be avoided.
- Attempt to extend deadlines (e.g. using phrases such as 'this will take time', 'others have to make this decision, 'I haven't the authority', 'I have to sell property to raise the funds', 'I cannot access this money' are helpful).
- Use active listening skills (paraphrasing, summarising, mirroring words used). Always show you are listening, confirm details.
- Avoid interrupting.
- Avoid making promises we cannot keep. Admit and explain difficulties in meeting demands.
- Reduce expectations and discuss the most achievable demand if many are made.
- Challenge any violence towards the hostage (e.g. 'this will not help your cause').
- Emphasise the positive actions we have taken to seek reciprocity.
- Remember that everyone is nervous, even the kidnappers. They may be brief and curtail the call. This is not a reflection on your ability; it may simply be to avoid

detection. No matter what, remember to tape or write a transcript of the call. Plan and prepare for the next one. Ensure silent running and have assistance with written prompts. Remember to vary the length of time you let the phone ring, but never fail to pick up.

Phew! Do all that and you are amazing. Do some of it and you will get by until negotiators arrive.

I issue instructions to the officer.

'It's best you hand him over to us for the next call. Introduce us to him. Tell him that we work for the police and will be talking to him from now on. This will probably upset him and he might want you to stay on the line. Refuse this and say that you have another role and that it will be our sole purpose to talk with him so that we can dedicate all our time to solving the incident and focussing on him. This will also send the message that we are in this for the long run and that he can't always have what he asks for.'

We sit in the armed response vehicle and plan for the next call. The officer tells me that he had several calls from a man called Eli, who sounded very wound up and who claimed to have a collection of bullets and weapons on his person. The fact that he had previously shot at armed police was proof of this. We were only a few hours into the incident by this point, hardly enough time for the suspect's intense emotion to have dissipated enough to allow us an opportunity to establish meaningful dialogue and problem solving.

The officer told me that Eli mainly shouts and is very *anti-police*. He also tells me that he holds a series of previous criminal convictions and that he is already wanted for pointing a firearm at an unarmed cop. Finally, he tells me that it had been impossible for him to build up any sort of rapport with the guy over the previous hours as he'd been so unbelievably angry on all previous calls.

After a few minutes of deliberation, my colleague and I come to a decision on the dialogue and strategy to use. We also decide to make use of the inside of the windows of the police car by sticking yellow 'Post-It' notes around the glass to transform it into a mobile negotiating cell.

The first call is always the hardest. *The Handover* as we like to call it. I waited with anticipation, expecting the shit to kick off at any minute. Eli had been speaking to one officer for a number of hours. Handing him over to a different person, a negotiator, would make him feel out of control. If he knew as much about the police as we presumed he did, he would know that we were trained negotiators, hoping to distance ourselves from the police and their tactics in order to gain trust. Trust that he would be very keen to avoid.

As my team mate and I discussed our plan of action, we decided to wait half an hour before ringing Eli. This will allow more time to plan and rehearse and think of suitable responses to potentially difficult questions. As we prepare, the activity surrounding the operation becomes more and more immense. Inner and outer cordons are set up. Armed marksmen are deployed into nearby buildings and on top of roofs. Key holders and landlords are contacted so that we can get a layout of the flat where Eli is hiding.

A new negotiating cell is identified and equipped so that we can move out of our armed vehicle and into more luxurious surroundings. This would also have a landline for better sound quality communication. In the surrounding area, local community leaders and resident housing associations are briefed to ensure the police maintain public confidence. Bus routes are altered. Media centres are created. Eli's history is examined and his relatives are identified for future possible intermediary negotiation. Anyone who says that managing a siege and negotiating is an easy and slow process, really has no idea of the sheer volume of activity that goes on behind the scenes.

I still remember the first phone call we had with Eli. The phone started ringing in the middle of our preparation, interrupting our flow. I could see the officer in front of me answering the phone, his forehead slowly creasing, his eyes widening; as if to indicate that this was him, this was *our* guy on the phone. There was a brief moment of tension. I could hear Eli's voice roaring through the receiver. On and on and on it went, a barrage of insults and aggravations streaming out through the mouthpiece. He was so enraged it was terrifying. I didn't know this guy and I didn't know what had made him act like this. It was clear to me that we were at the receiving end of a vicious force of anger that had clearly reached boiling point. I could see the armed response officer's brow getting tighter and tighter as the voice grew louder and louder. Eli must have tired himself out, because he hung up.

By this point, due to the cold winter air outside the vehicle, and the hot air being spoken inside of it, the atmosphere of our 'mobile cell' slowly resembled a steam room. I ring the boss to find out where we're at with our new working office. He tells me that he's managed to secure a location in a flat nearby which had been commandeered solely for our use. We set about safely vacating our hot, steamy vehicle and making our way over to a small block of flats.

We were greeted by my boss on the first floor, along with a flurry of technical bods running cables from each and every direction, like high tech ants on a mission to re-wire the colony. I knew the techies would be trying to get some sound and vision equipment into the stronghold to gain intelligence. They took our phones and plugged them into various sockets that would connect us to providers. Soon we would have a dedicated line between Eli and ourselves to prevent interruption and ensure that we're always able to communicate.

I glanced around the flat, a grey and dingy sort of place which had clearly been uninhabited for a long time. There was no furniture, no heating, no curtains, and no food. In other words, nothing remotely resembling human comfort.

Thirty minutes later, after spit-balling ideas on how best to handle the takeover, it was time to give Eli a call. The phone rang and we waited, the butterflies rising in my stomach. After what seemed like an eternity, Eli answered. We agreed that the officer will handover the communication to Rachel, my colleague, and I will be her coach.

E. What?

Good start.

N. Oh, hello Eli, I have some important information to explain to you.

E. Good for you, man.

N: I am going to hand you over to another officer. She will talk with you from now on.

E. She? A fucking woman? Where you off to?

Oh dear. Sexist and an attempted police killer. It seems this man has few redeeming qualities.

N. Well I have other roles to perform. I told you earlier that I am an armed officer. These guys are here and their sole role is to talk with you, to dedicate all their time to you. That's their job so someone will always be here on the phone to talk with you. OK?

E. No, it's not fucking OK. They have called in the professionals have they? The negotiators? Trying to psych me out with using their psychology on me? Like that will work? Bring it on.

Click. Phone down. That went well. It seems he's watched the films and knows all about negotiators. He's probably basing his knowledge on 'Proof of Life', where we go into the jungle on rescue missions. Or 'Man on Fire' where a lone man seeks out a kidnapped gang and at the very end hands himself in, in exchange for a kidnapped child. (Note to self: don't hand yourself in and avoid entering into jungle scenarios). On the plus side at least, both of these perceptions focus on the 'toughness' of negotiator squads so there's every chance that Eli now feels intimidated and is contemplating giving up. Unlikely.

I suggest to my colleague Rachel that she talks in an American accent and offers to trade her life in exchange for his release. She just glares at me with a 'don't be so stupid' expression that isn't too dissimilar from the one my wife uses. That's what I get for trying to make a joke and lighten the mood between negotiator calls.

Rachel and I decide to take matters into our own hands and let the previous armed cop go home. This sends the message to Eli that we are here to stay and that he can't decide who he wants to talk to. We thank the officer for a job well done, for his perseverance and for his ability in not getting shot by the vitriolic and violent individual who has been making his work life a living hell for the better part of a day.

We set about re-creating our mobile negotiation cell using the walls and windows of the apartment. We placed flip charts with useful headings on the walls. We agreed seating positions. And perhaps most importantly of all, we located the kettle. In those days we always worked in twelve hour shifts before handing over to a new set of negotiators. It was going to be a long evening and tea and coffee was of the utmost importance.

Over the next few hours we receive several calls from Eli, which are then met with long periods of silence. A summary of the call content could be described as tense at best. We were dealing with a man who despised the police and also knew a fair bit about the sort of work we did. On the phone he had claimed that he would 'never come out alive' and that if we wanted him, we'd have to 'come in and get him ourselves.' Statements like these had the phrase 'suicide cop' written all over them and we knew to tread carefully.

After an hour or so it appeared Eli had enough of talking to us. He was probably disappointed we were not going to storm the building, so he could go out in a blaze of glory. We repeatedly rang to no avail. My boss wanted us to keep trying every five minutes. Time went on, but as he continued to sulk and refuse to pick up his mobile, we decided that the best method of communication would be to venture out into the streets with body armour and ballistic shields and shout at him through a megaphone until he gave in and spoke to us. It was the coordinator's intention to keep him awake all night. Along with the neighbours. Not good for police relations during the season of good will.

There we were, standing in the freezing cold and shouting wildly through a megaphone. All in the hope that the crazy, hardened criminal hiding inside his flat would be persuaded into thinking that now would be an excellent time to 'come out.' It was getting dark by this point and the perfect opportunity for him to save face; no one would see him surrender if he chose to do so. By this point the streets had been cleared and some of the residents in the flats nearby had been evacuated.

Funny that normally we get criticised by the public when we storm premises to arrest people. But in this instance, we'd been receiving complaints for *not* doing so. The fact that it was freezing cold and the Christmas holidays might have contributed to this public shift in attitude. Nonetheless, local people were being filmed on national news and demanding that the police storm the building to 'take him out.' And they say the holidays bring out the best in people.

The evening turned into night, the night turned into the early hours of the morning before we were finally handed over to another negotiating team and I was allowed to drift off in search of some breakfast and some tea. I was to return the next day with a similar routine, following the tactic of 'don't let him sleep and make him uncomfortable.' Every time he refused to answer his phone, we were to traipse out into the freezing cold and demand that he answers it, shouting through our megaphones like some pushy human ring tone. The poor neighbours.

This went on for three days. At times he would pick up his mobile phone and at times he would ignore it. And it wasn't until day four, when we were looking back through our log entries and intelligence briefings, to see if we missed anything, when we saw recorded that one of the armed officers had reported the possibility of their being another person being holed up in the flat with Eli. He has apparently seen a shadow moving that was a body of smaller frame than our Eli.

At this moment we realised that our Eli never indicated whether or not he was alone. I decided it might be a good idea to ask him. Twenty minutes later, we were on the phone.

M. So Eli, do you have someone else in there with you?

E. Yep I do, you want to speak to him?

I'll admit, his answer shocked me a little. It's not every day that you find a kidnapper who's so ready and willing to let you speak to their hostage. Not only that, but we had been sitting here for four days without knowing that there was a possible hostage in there with him!

M. Yes please Eli that would be good.

I hear footsteps and some whispering and then we are handed over to a quietly spoken hostage, (H).

H. Hello?

M. Hey, so who are you?

H. Paul.

M. How are you Paul?

I'm not sure what sort of reply I expect to get from this question. 'Great thanks, never better' seems unlikely.

H. Not good man. I woke up this morning with a gun pointed at my head. He has a gun and loads of bullets.

M. OK, so you are being held in there against your will?

H. Course I am!

M. Listen Paul we have a large team out here doing everything they can to get you out.

H. Yeah right, you didn't even know I was in here!

Good point mate, can't argue with that.

M. Make sure you don't antagonise Eli, OK?

H. What does that mean?

M. Don't upset him.

Note to self, no big words for Paul.

H. He's the one with the gun. Listen, I can probably escape as he has only barricaded the back door with an old bicycle and furniture. I can move that quite quickly and make a break for it.

We don't usually say 'yes' or 'no' to a hostage who asks for advice on whether to escape; it's for them to decide. Our job is to point out the risks of such action. On this occasion however, I knew it would have been quite dangerous for Paul to suddenly run out. It was dark outside and the officers guarding the premises believed at this stage that the suspect was on his own inside the flat. If our Paul decided to leap out of the rear door running for help, arms waving, he might get shot. It was a risk we couldn't take.

M. Not now Paul. But let's focus on getting you out of there safely, Okay?

H. I think he is going to kill me. He keeps saying that he is going to shoot me.

M. Where is he now?

H. In another room.

At this point we thought it best to update the tactical commander that there may shortly be a screaming hostage running from the flat in pursuit of freedom. Meanwhile, we'd done everything we could think of to convince our hostage to stay put. For all we knew, Paul's plan to escape was a test by Eli to see whether we would encourage his hostage to act against him. Had it gone through, we would have ended up breaking whatever true rapport and trust we'd managed to build. We needed to stay privy to any potential trickery.

M. So Paul, can you hand the phone back to Eli, please?

H. He's counting bullets.

That's not a good sign.

M. Oh Okay, and where might they be?

H. On top of a fridge in the kitchen, in a big bag.

In a big bag? How many bullets has this guy got?

M. How about you distract his counting bullets time and get him back on the phone to talk to us?

H. OK.

More whispering is heard.

E. Hi.

M. Hello again, Eli, listen, thank you for allowing us to talk to Paul there. Are you making sure he is safe in there with you?

E. He's fine and won't get hurt if you don't upset me.

P. That's good news. So anyway, have you given anymore thought about when you might be ready to come out?

E. No.

And with that, he hung up the phone.

The remainder of our twelve-hour shift remained fairly uneventful. We had a few more 'when are you coming out' chats followed by several longer chats about the sad life Eli had led (his words, not ours) and how we couldn't possibly understand where he was coming from. We showed empathy where we could and cooed appropriately over his past grievances, but when I went back home that night and thought about what I had achieved during the day, the only thing I could think of was that I'd managed to speak to a hostage and convince him not to escape.

I tried unsuccessfully to sleep for at least a few hours, knowing that the following day it would start all over again.

At some point in the early hours of the morning, having only been asleep for three hours, the phone rang. It was the negotiating coordinator (my boss) ringing from the scene.

'Hi Martin, can you make your way to Edmonton Police Station and de-brief the hostage that escaped from Eli?'

Ah. Clearly Paul had listened carefully to my advice on staying put. I must hone my persuasion skills, because you may have noticed throughout this book, they haven't always been that successful, if at all. I find myself wondering how Eli found out about the escape and how upset he would now be with the current negotiator. I then find myself feeling very grateful that I'm not the one on duty and having to placate him.

I arrive at the police station some time later and I am shown into a small room where Paul is sat looking (understandably) shaken. He's wearing one of those white paper onesies that we dress people in when we need their clothes for forensics. (Looking back, I think the police came up with this fashion trend before anyone else did. I know ours is missing the fluffy ear and tail ensemble, but other than that we had the basics covered).

I introduce myself to Paul who stands up dazedly and shakes my hand.

'Hi Paul, I'm Martin, the negotiator you spoke to yesterday. I advised you not to escape when we spoke on the phone yesterday afternoon as we hadn't briefed the inner armed containment and we also assumed that Eli was listening in on our call. We are always conscious that a hostage may be forced to say things to us to test us or put us under pressure. I hope you understand?'

I look at Paul and wait for a response. He looks back at me with total confusion then smiles and shrugs, clearly happy enough in the knowledge that he's free and that, for now, nothing else really matters.

I decide to stop being technical and start being friendly. I ask him if he's being well looked after and whether or not he'd like something to eat.

'I'm a bit hungry,' Paul admits.

'Great,' I say, 'so what do you fancy? Obviously it's all on us and you can take your pick from any of the restaurants on the high street.'

He beams back at me, 'A Kentucky chicken and Coke would be great, man.'

I remember smiling at that. It had seemed mildly comical that after nearly escaping death, KFC would have been Paul's dinner of choice. I guess in Paul's case comfort food was chicken in a bucket.

We sent out for food, and Paul sat there eating it from a white paper bag, dressed in his white paper suit, feeling like he was the centre of attention. Which, to be honest, he was. He was the surviving hostage of the UK's longest running siege. After he'd eaten his weight in chicken wings, Paul and I sat together and he told me what had happened in the flat with Eli. He told me he'd often woken up with a gun pointing at his head and that he'd stayed confined to his bedroom as much as possible, being too afraid to go out and talk to Eli. After a while he'd decided he'd had enough and as Eli had seemed like he was becoming more unstable. He decided to make a break for it and get out of the flat. He gave us some detail about the firearms and ammunition Eli held, as well as the conversations he'd had with him when the negotiators had finished their calls. It was all vital information that we could use to our advantage.

I fed back a summary of the de-brief to the negotiating coordinator and then took leave for a few days. It was New Year after all. I took some earned leave and went off with my family to the coast to forget about the last few days. I imagined that it should be over soon. I saw on the news that the police were delivering food to him by hoisting a plastic chest up by rope to his flat. I had also heard that we had cut all the power to the flat as a tactic to ensure he was very cold and miserable and which would hopefully force him to come out. It was a particularly cold few days so that would increase the discomfort. You can imagine my surprise when, after taking leave for two days, I received a call asking me to go back to Hackney and return to the scene to negotiate. I was dumbfounded. The average length of a siege in the UK is seven hours. This one had been running for almost a week!

On my return there followed a couple of 12 hour shifts during which time we managed to make no real progress. Most of us believed that he had gone too far now and there was no way back for him. He knew he was going to prison for a long time. We brought relatives to talk with him, to no avail. Eventually I was relieved of duty by a different team of negotiators and the incident was brought to a close on their shift. The result was a sad one and even I felt some pity for Eli. He was eventually shot by armed police, having set fire to his flat in a last act of desperation. He was confirmed as deceased some time later when it was safe for emergency services to enter. We had tried very hard to empathise with him and get him to give himself up. We were however unsuccessful.

Text on the move

This is a story that brings the Metropolitan Police into the 21st century. Before you ask, no we are not implementing the use of hover boards, but rather the act of negotiating via SMS, at a time prior to smartphones.

This sort of negotiating is becoming more common as predominantly, young millennials find it easier to communicate their feelings in print rather than in person.

This particular case had us attempting to locate a young suicidal man who was driving around London on an emotional rampage, whilst communicating with his best mate via a mobile phone.

This had its advantages, as we were able to sit with the friend and advise him on what to type. Our person in a crisis meanwhile had no idea that the messages he was receiving were from a law enforcement officer.

The suicidal man in question was going through something of a rough patch. He claimed that his girlfriend had ended their long-term relationship and he claimed he now planned to overdose before crashing his car deliberately into a wall or driving off a bridge. It was all quite dramatic.

The call initially came to us from the ex-girlfriend, Sally. She stated that her ex-boyfriend, Bret, (who had a long-standing drug habit) was threatening to commit suicide after she'd ended their fractious relationship that day. It was all quite raw for our Bret.

When she called us for help, she mentioned that Bret's best friend Guy had already received some worrying text messages from him, hinting that he might be about to take his own life. We made our way over to Guy's flat in East London and asked him first-hand what contact he'd received. Sure enough, we found a smattering of sad (and fairly incomprehensible) text messages on Guy's phone, spouting vitriol about 'giving up' and 'reaching the end.'

Guy agreed to let us reply to the messages on his phone and see if we could talk some sense in to young Bret. We also sent for officers to bring the (now ex) girlfriend Sally over to the flat also. This was in case Bret tried to make contact with her during his mini-rampage.

There we all were, sat in Guy's kitchen with two mobile phones, a negotiating team and horrible instant coffee.

I continued to look at the previous text messages from Bret. They were mostly along the lines of *'I can't go on without her'* and *'I'm taking tabs man, don't bother tryin to stop me.'* The replies that Guy sent back had been un-insightful, things like *'She ain't worth it, bro'* and *'plenty more fish, dude.'* They weren't quite the replies we learned at Negotiating School, but it did give us some insight into the sort of language Guy used, which would help us later when we were crafting our replies and pretending to be him.

Most people know that the police can trace mobile phones, but it does have its limitations, especially if the phone in question is moving within built-up areas in a vehicle. Bret was out there in London, driving around to his heart's content, but to get an accurate reading on where he was, we needed him to either remain stationary, or go to a place where he could be intercepted.

Our main strategy was to minimise the risk to the general public and to Bret. Driving around in an irrational state whilst on drugs did not make him the safest person to get behind a wheel. We needed our communication and wording to cause him to reflect on this point and hopefully stop driving.

As we huddled around the kitchen table, sipping instant Nescafe and waiting for the phones to ring, I set about writing scripts for Guy and Sally to spin into their own vocabulary. They were fairly generic messages, and I noted each of them with bullet points.

- We want you to stay safe.
- Please think about stopping your car when you communicate
- Everyone is really worried about you.
- Where are you heading?
- What are you planning?
- We are here to talk face to face, so please come and talk.
- We are listening.
- You sound really upset, tell me about it.

I told Guy and Sally to be wary of intelligence gathering and to listen out for noises like trains, planes, traffic, birds, lions, or any other outside sounds that came to them down the phone. If he did happen to call all of this evidence would give us some clue as to where Bret was, be it a station, café or zoo.

In the time since we arrived in the kitchen, Bret hadn't sent one text message. He also hadn't bothered contacting Sally, which seemed strange to me. She was after all, the one who had set this 'Thelma and Louise'-like debacle into action.

I asked Sally about their relationship. By all accounts it didn't sound like it had been a great one. They'd been together for about a year and in that time had had lots of fights and separations. I told Sally that she didn't need to feel guilty about what was currently unfolding. Judging by the accounts of Bret's character, I figured this sort of cry for help had always been on the cards. The drug taking and his inability to hold down work had merely set the wheels in motion. The guy probably suffered from a serious lack of self-worth. Our tactic was to remind Bret that he was special and loved. Looking around the table though it was clear this wasn't the case in this kitchen. Sally had spent the last half hour complaining about the fact she was stuck in some house with two cops she didn't know. All she wanted to do was go home, watch daytime television and read magazines. Guy on the other hand was miffed because he'd had to cancel a day's labouring due to Bret's drama. He told us he didn't want to be here as he thought that Bret was 'a bit of a knob anyway.' It wasn't the most optimistic of situations, but then you have to work with what you've got.

We circulated Bret's car details to various police units in the vicinity. We established a list of the places he might visit, his knowledge of London, what he was wearing and the contact details of friends and family in London.

We waited for another half an hour and eventually, an SMS came through on Guy's phone.

'Yo man, I can't go on.'

Roughly translated, this could mean *'Hello Guy, I'm going to commit suicide.'*

Active listening in print can be hard, but we can still apply the usual conversation rules such as taking turns, leaving the right length of pause, reflecting, mirroring language and using emotional labelling. There is also some thought in the Neuro Linguistic Programming world that we use language in accordance with the communicating/learning style we prefer, be it visual, auditory or kinaesthetic.

Visual learners watch and remember what was seen. They are less distracted by noise and are predominantly more observant.

Auditory learners are easily distracted. They learn by listening and like verbal instruction. They read aloud, they are talkative, they remember what was discussed and they remember names.

Kinaesthetic learners touch and stand close. They point when reading, respond to physical rewards, move a lot, learn by doing and often use gestures to remember what was done.

I never use this theory of learning preference when negotiating, but I have used it when replying to emails and to good effect. By that I mean it has been useful in building rapport and influence.

Have a look at the examples below, which are an amalgamation of language used by people in emails, who clearly have a strong preference for either visual, audio of kinaesthetic language.

- Visual: *'I don't see how accepting this offer moves me any further forward. It's the same vision of the future as before. Can you show me how things have changed?'*

- Auditory: *'I hear what you're saying but the terms are not sounding right. I would like to listen to some other alternatives.'*

- Kinesthetic: *'I sense your company has presented the facts but they have left me feeling a bit cold. Is there another way we can tackle this?'*

As an exercise for you the reader, it might be worth trying to fashion a reply to these emails using the preference language used by the author.

For now though, let's turn back to the story.

By this point, I was thinking it would be a good idea to get Bret on the phone and talking, so that we could understand his mood, build rapport, gain intelligence and prevent misunderstandings. I fashioned a first response for Guy to send:

'Dude, why don't you ring me? I want to talk to you.'

By sending this, we might get the reason for why he wouldn't speak in person.

We send the message from Guy's phone, then sit and wait, hoping he'll ring. After we send the message, Guy tells me that he tried to ring Bret a number of times but that he ignored every call. Like I said earlier, people find it easier to talk about their emotions in a remote fashion. Whereas talking face to face puts people under pressure. This accounts for why we all sound so much angrier on Twitter and other social media, where *everyone seems outraged at everything!* It's easier to demonstrate anger at someone who isn't there. After ten minutes we get another text. It isn't wildly interesting:

'Mte just text, feelin like the end, nuff said.'

We assume this means, '*I don't want to talk anymore as I am going to commit suicide.*'

I contemplate sending a *sad face* emoji as a response but think better of it. I glance at Sally. She's drumming her pink, painted fingernails on the table, clearly not giving a toss as to whether Bret lives or dies. Guy on the other hand, has a fairly caring expression on his face. He asks me what the next step should be.

Through some forced chatter, we establish that Bret likes taking uppers, downers, skank, blow, puff, weed and ecstasy. Basically, anything that makes him feel better than how he actually feels. No one knew what substances he'd taken on this day, but his past history of substance abuse didn't bode well for us. We essentially had a spaced out, suicidal driver on the loose, so we needed to be proactive by calling and sending texts. At the very least that would keep him awake. We try calling Bret from Guy's phone. He doesn't answer. We try calling from Sally's phone. Again, he doesn't answer. We follow up Sally's call with a text message:

'*Guy has called me, what's going on? x* '

Perhaps Bret would become more flexible if he knew that Guy and Sally were communicating with each other. Another half an hour went by and we were back to silence and wonder. Where was Bret? Would he actually drive in to a wall? Were we doing enough to find him? Why does Guy make such awful coffee? How much more hair product can Sally put in her hair? As I sit pondering the answer to these questions, another message comes through, this time to Sally:

'*Dnt txt me bitch I no u dnt wnt me ur loss.*'

Roughly translated:

'Please don't text me Sally. It is clear for all to see that you no longer wish for us to be an item. Kindest regards.'

We reply with the following:

'I am worried about u babe please ring me or Guy. We both care about u x'

We hope the 'babe' and 'x' will convince Bret that Sally cares. In reality, Sally doesn't give a jot, as evidenced by the fairly un-inspiring conversation that we then share with Sally in the kitchen.

Me. So what sort of relationship did you have with Bret, Sally?

Sally. A shit one.

Me. Do you think you will get back together?

Sally: No fucking chance.

Me. Do you think that he thinks you will?

Sally. If he's deluded.

Me. Do you think he will actually kill himself?

Sally. Hope so.

Need I go on? At the very least, Sally was here with us, helping the Met's finest save a life, a life which in her opinion, wasn't really worth saving. Guy on the other hand, still looked genuinely worried and seemed to believe that his knob of a friend would actually drive into a wall and carry out his threat.

Apparently, Bret had already tried to kill himself once before but had failed because the drugs he had tried to overdose on were not what he thought they were. (He thought he was taking Paracetamol, in fact they were indigestion tablets. At the very least, Bret would have died with an acid free stomach).

Guy's phone beeps again. It's another message from Bret. It reads:

'Bro that bitch is working with the cops. She never normally cares, tell me the truth. Are they with you? That's betrayal if you no what I mean.'

Bugger. It seemed Sally's message had sounded too emotional. Clearly, we hadn't pitched it right. And clearly Bret doesn't know how to spell or punctuate. I decided it was best to be truthful. For all we knew, Bret could have been spying on us through the kitchen window this whole time. We might as well be honest.

I ask Guy to send the following message:

'Mate, I was really worried and didn't know what to do. I called the police as I wanted them to find you quicker than I could, to keep you safe. '

We receive a reply back:

'Traitor thought u wuz a mte.'

Guy sends the following:

'It's because I am a mate that I did this. Tell me where you are so we can help you.'

Bret replies with:

'Everyone seems to lie to me and now even you.'

Guy: 'We want to help you. If you are driving, stop for a moment to think. You have lots of mates that will miss you. The police only want to help. You are not in any trouble.'

Bret: 'Fuck them. They will stich me up for something.'

There is sadly some truth in Bret's response. Not that we plan to stitch him up, but he will probably get nicked for drug driving (assuming he is on drugs at this point and not indigestion tablets). If he is over the limit or impaired, that certainly won't help his case either.

I continue to advise what to put into the text messages, so Guy can translate into youth speak, in'it.

Guy: *'Can we talk about this mate. I am always here. I can come and met you somewhere.'*

Bret: *'Like fuck and bring the filth with you.'*

Guy: *'No just me they said I can come alone.'*

Bret: *'Like I should believe you, and you have always fancied Sal.'*

Ah, here we go. Jealous and distrusting and now he hates his best mate. At this point, I decide to check on other police action to see if they've had any luck in tracking Bret down. They haven't. We persevere.

Guy: *'Have you taken anything mate? I don't want you injuring yourself. The police have said they will get a doctor to you and get you to hospital if necessary. They are not interested in arresting you or anything. Sally is still your friend also. '*

In a situation like this, we could again be in a 'saving face' scenario. Bret has cried for help but now has no real intention of carrying out his suicide threat. He now needs a way out to save his 'rep,' so to speak, particularly in front of Sally. On first impressions she seems to have been out with everyone on the street and doesn't look much like the loyal type. (As evidenced by Sally and Guy themselves, who have been holding hands under the table for the majority of the debacle and talking about going out for a drink when 'all this shit, is like, over.')

I decide to pause on the texts as we don't seem to be getting anywhere. But a moment later, Sally's phone rings. 'It's him!' she squeals. I frantically push my scripts under her nose. She frowns at me, storms out of the kitchen, runs upstairs and locks herself in the bathroom. With the mobile phone. All I hear as she legs it up the stairs are sentences like 'Wanker, what did you expect?' and 'Of course I do' and 'No, they made me' and 'No, he's just a mate. Where are you?'

I go upstairs and knock on the bathroom door. I don't want to shout in case Bret can hear me, but things are beginning to get out of control. Sally doesn't answer the door but continues talking to Bret.

After five minutes I sense things are getting calmer as she stops shouting and starts speaking in a more mellow tone. Progress, I think. Perhaps she's memorised my carefully crafted scripts and is reciting them down the phone word for word. Suddenly, we hear a loud crash from downstairs. I run downstairs to find the kitchen window now smashed into shards, with a half of a brick lying amongst the debris. Has Bret been watching us this whole time? Surely not.

I run outside but can't see anyone so go back inside to Sally to monitor the call. I can hear her shouting 'Was that you, you wanker!' amongst several other loud profanities, which I won't bother repeating. I wait patiently to see how the event unfolds. Eventually, Sally emerges from the bathroom and hands me the mobile, informing me that Bret has hung up on her and that she now needs to go to the loo and can she have some privacy please?

I ring my colleague at the local police department and inform them of what's going on, asking them to send some uniform units to assist with the search for Bret. It doesn't take them long to find him. Eventually a uniformed cop comes to the door and tells us that Bret was found rolling around on the neighbour's lawn, clearly high on some drug and shouting obscenities at all and sundry. He was later arrested for trying to punch my colleague. I saw Sally run out angrily into the street to confront him about his behaviour, but alas, all she got was the sight of Bret in handcuffs being put into the back of a police vehicle and driven off to face the music.

We were duped and he was watching us for some of the time. I reckon to test his relationships with Guy and Sally. I was annoyed that the uniform police, parked in the street, had not noticed him arrive. I was also annoyed that we had been caught out. I was annoyed with Sally for going off script and running off. I was just annoyed all round really. At least no one was killed and we got our man off the street. I just hoped our texts went someway in delaying his intended actions and will make him think about his future in a more positive light. Another negotiated result which involved people being thrown to the floor. I don't think I am very good at this.

Fish in a Barrel

This incident takes place in a secure ward of a large North London Hospital. The hospital doubled up as unit that catered for those requiring help with mental health issues.

As a young Police Constable this was the hospital where we used to take those 'deemed to need medical help' for various psychiatric conditions. We would be tasked to take them there for compulsory assessments. Often we would take them in a police van and drop them off in the reception area. Some of the hospital wards were open for the patients to come and go with little supervision. At times on arrival we were greeted by doctors and patients and at times it was hard to recognize which was which. Some of the doctors were very eccentric.

The incident I'm about to recall occurred late one night and involved a young, mentally ill patient called Colin. Colin had cunningly obtained a set of keys to a secure ward within the psychiatric hospital before ushering the staff out and locking the door and all the patients inside of it. It wasn't ideal, particularly as most of the patients trapped inside suffered from fairly severe psychiatric conditions, the symptoms of which only started to escalate if they missed a dose of their appropriate medication. Colin used his intelligence and barricaded the door with heavy beds in case there was a spare key.

On arrival I was briefed by the negotiator coordinator, the local uniformed inspector and the doctor on call. I was informed that the patient, Colin, was a long-term patient who suffered from schizophrenia. He required several drugs to maintain some form of equilibrium and could be quite agitated if he missed a dose, or things didn't go quite his way. In the ward with him were six other patients all suffering from similar disorders. On the day in question there was apparently nothing out of the ordinary in Colin's manner, but when the ward doctor was leaving, he was threatened by Colin with a photograph of a dog and a bunch of flowers. (Apparently, according to the doctor, there were thorns on the flower stems and the photo was in a very sharp looking frame). Being attacked by a knife would make for a better story down the pub. *'So what happened at the hospital Jim, I hear you were attacked at work?' 'Yeah he came at me with a daffodil with huge petals and he was also waving a picture of a Labrador in my face.'* The doctor was *allegedly* pinned to the wall and ordered to hand over the keys. He duly handed them over and was ushered outside.

The inspector informed me that a local uniform cop had been talking to Colin through the glass panel in the door to the ward. Colin had been unresponsive but could be seen talking with the other patients and carrying on as though nothing had happened.

(In his head, perhaps, nothing had!) I was told that the glass was reinforced and that if we shouted he can hear us. Great, more shouting whilst trying to build rapport. Never a good thing.

I approached the door where I nodded to the uniform cop. I looked through the glass partition. Most of the patients were lying on their beds, either reading books or staring at nothing in particular. They looked pretty safe, dare I say happy, which didn't really bode well for us at our end. Nothing screams 'long drawn out negotiation' like a group of people who aren't in danger. It occurred to me then that most of the patients in there probably didn't even know that they were being held hostage. And judging by the serene expressions on their faces, at this point we couldn't justify breaking the door down.

'I've been shouting for hours,' the uniform cop told me. 'So far I've just been ignored. Although every now and then the patients come past the glass, bend over and...' He trailed off at this point and gestured to the glass panel, behind which several semi-nude patients were bent over, arses in the air, waving their hips backwards and forwards in our direction.

In Summary, not much progress.

I asked the doctor whether Colin had access to his medication and was informed that all medication is locked away in another secure location outside of this ward. I reflected back to what I was told on arrival and asked what will happen if the patients cannot access their medication and how long we have before we may notice behavioral changes that could affect our progress? 'It varies' I was informed. 'Some in there get very anxious, some get violent, some depressed and then there are those that become suicidal' Great, so a full house of issues that looks like a powder keg ready to explode in our faces. 'How long have we got before everyone morphs into our worst nightmare?' I ask.

'Probably until the morning, as most will miss their evening medication if the situation doesn't change.'

I do hope I am not still here in the morning.

I begin my attempt to prevent chaos in the early hours by beginning my Jedi like negotiation. I stepped forward and shouted through the glass panelling.

M. Hello?

Nothing.

M. Hello?

Nothing.

M. Colin can you hear me?

Nothing. This is painful.

M. Colin, listen we need to discuss where you see this going, we are not going away until you talk with us. We are very concerned about you and the others in there with you.

Plus, if you don't have your medication, it will be nigh on impossible for me to negotiate with you. So, get chatty, mate.

At this point two of the other patients walk up to me at the glass partition. One then puts his lips against the glass and blows hard so his cheeks expand out like a Puffa fish. He backs up leaving lip shaped marks on the window and the other one turns away and shows me his hairy arse. Don't you just love this job?

M. Guys that's not helping.

At this point it seems I am talking to the inhabitants of an aquarium as several decide to do the Puffa fish impersonation up at the glass. I feel like a dentist examining the inside of their mouths as they take great pleasure in kissing the glass.

At least they all don't line up and bare bums to impersonate a bike rack. Things are looking up.

My concern with this situation is not so much Colin and his wanderings, it's the other patients and what they may do if they become frustrated and impatient with Colin and his intentions. If they are prevented from their daily doses how will they react? As soon as any violence is imminent, we will have to attempt entry to save lives. That said, we can't enter in quick time by this door as it's barricaded. We would require a hydraulic device that we use to expand the door frame, so we can pop off the hinges by either a crow bar or Hatton rounds fired from a shotgun. I doubt whether any of this action will allay the fears of the ward residents. Shotguns and noisy hydraulics don't normally make for a calm environment!

I assume the local Inspector is planning for this eventuality and calling in firearms support that possess this equipment. He will also require the public order unit on standby to enter with protective shields should violence ensue. In fact, he requires half of the Met's finest, quite a lot of resources, briefed and on standby. He will then have to decide when, if and who shall enter. Big decisions to make, as people tend to get hurt one way or another when such tactics are deployed. Sometimes due to no fault of anyone, just circumstance.

Anyway, all of that is not my concern. My priority is to prevent use of force happening and get Colin to open the door so we can end this incident in a peaceful and calm way. Then we can all go home and have our dinner.

M. Colin? I am here to listen and help. What made you lock the door today and take the keys? I appreciate that you are keeping everyone in there with you safe.

I also appreciate the fact you haven't impersonated a creature of the deep yet or shown me your arse. Yet.

M. Come on Colin this can be solved and nothing bad will happen to you or anyone in there. If you are frustrated with something, we can talk about it and see if we can sort it.

I would like some more intelligence at this point. For example, details of his family, his likes, dislikes, how long he has been in hospital, some life history, *anything!* I decide to walk away and approach the police makeshift control room in the reception. I ask the coordinator for the above information. It seems he has no family. He has been in and out of mental institutions most of his life. He has attempted suicide many times and needs medication to protect him from severe delusional episodes. As far as candidates for negotiation go, Colin was proving to be a bit of a toughie.

I wander back over to the door and peer through the glass. There's been little change. I wonder what my next move should be. An important part of negotiating is mirroring body language as it helps to build rapport. I contemplate pressing my mouth up against the glass 'Puffa fish' style but then quickly decide against it. I shout through the glass:

M. Colin, look we are here until you open the door.

At this point, one of the patients approaches the glass. He looks at me and smiles happily.

M. Hi who are you?

T. Terry, so what's happening?

M. Maybe you can tell me, where is Colin and what's his issue today?

T. He is lying down on his bed around the corner I think he is asleep.

M. Do you know where the keys are?

T. No.

M. Would you ask Colin to come and talk with me please?

T. OK.

That was easy... remember though...'Just when you think you are winning.'

C. (Shouting from out of sight) who the fuck said you could talk to those wankers?!

Told you. But if nothing else Colin has decided to exercise his vocal chords at last. I must take advantage.

M. Is that Colin?

C. Is that Colin, is that Colin?

That's what I said.

M. Yes is that Colin?

C. Is that Colin?

Interesting conversation, I sense that this could go on for a while. I make an assumption that yes; it is in fact, Colin.

M. Hello Colin.

C. Who you calling Colin?

Whoops.

M. Then who are you and what is it that has made you question why this man at the door can talk to me?

C. What?

Admittedly that was a very complicated sentence.

M. Who are you?

C. Who are *you*?

M. My name is Martin; I am working with the police out here and would like you to please open this door.

C. My name is Martin and I am with the police.

M. Correct.

C. We are all fine in here so piss off, Martin with the police.

M. We can't go.

C. Has anyone been hurt, does everyone look happy in here?

M. People seem fine, but they might want to –

C. We are locked in here all day anyway so there is actually no difference. The only difference is we are not letting anyone in here to be with us because we want some us time.

He has a logical point, but is not seeing the bigger picture, and don't get me started on us *time. I actually don't know if he is being sarcastic or genuine with his replies.*

M. I think people in there would rather the door wasn't barricaded. And we may need to enter to cater for your welfare.

C. I have asked everyone in here and they agree with me, we want to be alone for a while.

M. How long are you thinking?

C. As long as we want.

It was becoming increasingly clear to me that Colin is not only educated, but he was able to communicate in a mellow, relaxed, coherent way. He didn't seem nervous. In fact, he seemed completely calm about the situation. Ironically, this was turning out to be one of the sanest negotiations I'd ever had to navigate. The fact that Colin had the patients on his side only made the situation trickier. He was a hostage taker without any real hostages.

C. I know you won't come in unless there is violence, so you won't come in. When we need our medication you can deliver it somehow and when we want food you can do likewise. But, if anyone should think about trying to take us on, there will be trouble, get it?

M. I think so, it appears you are set for a while, but you haven't told me why?

C. You are right I haven't.

M. So?

C. You are right I haven't.

And with that he turns on his heels and walks away from the door and out of sight around the corner. Why is it that everyone I talk to in this line of work is so bloody difficult??

M. (I shout after him) Colin? Colin, can you come back and talk to me please?

Nothing.

I decide to walk back to reception to brief my coordinator. As I arrive, I notice a flurry of activity. Firearms teams in ballistic vests and helmets are all in small huddles discussing sexy tactics and public order officers are strutting about pushing each other in the chest and farting. As negotiators we are never told when it's decided to *go tactical*. The reason for this, is because we may inadvertently alert the person we are talking to and compromise the operation in some way. If I knew that the police were about to crash through a window and subdue you in five minutes, I might give it away by glancing at the window or have an air of anticipation in my voice. The slightest change in my tone, pace of speech or change in body language may cause the person to be suspicious. If that's what is being discussed with the local Inspector I don't want to know and so I head back to the door without briefing my boss. Not that there was much to say anyway, other than the fish are all quiet in the aquarium and trousers are secure around waists.

I needed a new plan of attack as all this shouting was getting tiring. As I returned, I was followed by the coordinator. 'Martin, the doc says we need to give some of the patients their medication or some will panic. We are thinking of forcing the door open and those that need their tablets can come to the barricade and take them from us. We need you to explain this to Colin.' 'I am sure he will be overjoyed at that plan', I reply. 'Just do your best mate'

Here goes nothing.

M. Colin we are concerned that people in there with you need their medication before bed. So, we are going to take this door off its hinges and supply them. We are not coming in, we are just concerned about you and the others. We want everyone to remain calm in there, I promise we are not coming in, OK?

I look through the glass. There appears to be a meeting going on and Colin is chairing it. All the patients are standing in a tight circle, dressed in pyjamas, brows furrowed. It's bizarre to watch. I see Colin come to the glass.

C. You will probably switch our drugs and give us sleeping tablets, we are not buying it. I think we can do without them tonight.

I look at the others and it's clear that some look anxious at the thought of missing a dose and I decide to exploit that.

M. Colin it looks as though the others are worried about that prospect, think about them.

The meeting appears to be getting heated now and I suspect that Colin is losing some support. Three patients walk away from the main group and approach the door. One shouts, 'we agree'

C. No you fucking don't.

This isn't looking good. Colin marches up to the door and pulls the traitors away and pushes them in the chest back to his makeshift boardroom, shouting at them in the process. He does seem to have some hold over these guys.

M. Colin look what is happening. People want and need their tablets. The longer they go without them the more agitated they will become. I am also worried about you, do you know what happens to you if you miss a dose?

C. Yeah, I turn into a pumpkin.

Then come out here and try on this slipper Cinderella, and if it fits, we will supply you with Prozac.

M. Colin at the very least if the door comes off we can talk more easily, rather than all this shouting.

Someone shouts from the back of the room 'Father Christmas plays a saxophone'

I think it might be medication time.

From the back of the ward, more shouting, *'You don't get custard when the sun shines.'*

More shouting. 'snakes and ladders'

Oh dear.

During this time the coordinator was standing on my shoulder listening. No doubt admiring my ability at stirring up the incident and agitating everyone inside. I would add that it was *his* plan, I was just the messenger, so don't shoot me. 'right' he says and marches back to the macho brigade back at reception. I think I know what's going to happen.

M. Colin I think we are going to take this door off and then we can talk more easily. No one is coming in. It's better for all and then we can also pass you a cup tea or something, what do you say? Eh? Come on, makes sense yeah?

At this point one of the other patients starts banging his head against one of the walls, one kicks the TV and the Puffa fish impressions begin again at the door.

Arrrrrghhhhh, I am crap at this!

M. Colin people listen to you, can you try and calm people down.

C. What am I? A fucking doctor?

For all I know that's a possibility in this place mate.

M. They listen to you mate, its clear you are in charge in there. They respect you.

'No, we don't' someone. Shouts.

Great now I am turning them on one another. This is going so well. I am sure that if we hadn't turned up they would have all got bored and decided to open the door when they wanted their drugs. At times all we seem to do is antagonise situations and make matters worse. I suppose the reason we remain on scene is because we have a duty of care. Human rights and all that.

I can hear muffled tones behind me and heavy footsteps. Yup, as expected, here comes the cavalry. The two biggest officers are carrying a hydraulic ram and a metal battering ram for the door.

'Out the way mate,' one instructs me. I step to the side and admire how quickly the door is dispatched and we are now staring at a framed opening and a pile of stacked up furniture.

M. Colin, as promised we are staying this side of the door. No one is coming in. This is better now don't you agree?

Suddenly the three Puffa fish make a break for freedom and climb over the barricade into the arms of the uniformed cops. Colin is losing his hostages in quick time.

M. There you go Colin, it seems people did want their medication and were not happy being in there with you. Maybe now is the time to remove this furniture and come out?

It's at this point that I can't see Colin and this worries me. Once he realizes that he has lost control it's a worrying time for all.

M. Colin where have you gone?

M. Colin look some of the patients have decided to leave, why don't you help to move this barricade and follow suit, nothing will happen to you, it's all been forgotten OK?

I am conscious that now he needs to save face, as his plan, if he had one, has not been successful.

As I shout to 'invisible Colin' the remaining patients clamber over the furniture and towards the waiting police cordon. We confirm numbers with the staff and conclude that the only person left in the ward is Colin. If I was in charge I wouldn't wait too long for Colin to respond as he was out of view and could be self-harming. Particularly as he may see no way out now, losing any leverage he may have had with his hostages. But I am not in charge and leave such decisions up to the local Inspector. That's the problem, sometimes when you are negotiating you may have far more experience than the scene commander and you may be of a much higher rank. Your job though is to remain separated from any decision making.

I persevered for ten minutes attempting to get Colin to respond. Then as expected, a decision is taken to move me forward behind a team of officers carrying protective shields. I explain to Colin what is happening, so he won't freak out when we turn the corner and confront him. The barricade is removed and we advance to the corner in formation. It's awfully quiet I remember thinking; I do hope he is OK.

What I didn't expect to see was Colin naked and masturbating on his bed. So now I have seen it all. Arses, mouth cavities and now penises. What do you do or say in this situation? Not my usual 'Hi Colin my name is Martin and I am here to help' as that could be misunderstood. I thought about; 'This must be hard for you Colin' but again a double entendre was not appropriate. So, I settled on 'I was worried about you Colin, but clearly things are OK with you right now' He looked over and smiled and carried on as if we weren't even there. The sergeant in charge of the shield unit decided he couldn't watch this spectacle any longer and slowly approached with two of his men who broke away for the formation. They took hold of Colin's hands and secured him on his bed. The doctor followed us in and sat on Colin's bed as his penis and frustration at today's event subsided.

Colin never mentioned why he took the actions that day.

No more mistakes and the final chapter?

Throughout this book I have has shown you how, we in the emergency services, can sometimes use humour to alleviate the stresses of dealing life and death situations. Without humour to resort to, this job would slowly kill you.

This coping mechanism never distracts us from the severity of the issue in front of us. We deal with every incident passionately and professionally, keeping the wellbeing of the person in crisis front of mind at all times. We never forget that kidnappers are holding vulnerable and scared people captive, who we need to be released and returned to their loved ones.

As negotiators the variety of our work is constant. We go from dealing with violent criminals to lonely and suicidal individuals. The ability be flexible, adapt and overcome in each situation is key, for each case requires respect and understanding to enable us to effectively influence the individual and guide them towards a course of action what we're suggesting.

That said, we're all human and sometimes mistakes happen. Unfortunately, unlike the typical work place errors, our mistakes cost a lot more than a lost client or a late deadline proposal.

The first mistake I remember making as a coordinator negotiator was during an incident where my team of negotiators were trying to persuade a young man to come down from the roof of an apartment block. It was the typical 'I'm going to jump' routine and my team had already talked and listened through seven hours of mind numbing, futile dialogue. We'd done everything in our power to get him to come down and in the end thinking that he might actually jump, we'd asked a TV stunt company nearby to come over and place a pile of cardboard boxes onto the concrete that was surrounding the building. If he were to jump, he might have a chance of survival this way. I supervised the crew as they began piling box after box around the base of the building, I heard a shout from the roof. I looked up to see our man in question craning over the edge to take a look at the scene, a perturbed expression etched over his face.

'What are you doing?' he shouted. 'What are them boxes about?'

'They're to stop you from breaking your neck if you fall.' My negotiator replied.

I saw the dim dawn of realisation spread over the guy's face, if he jumped, he'd might end up dead or paralysed.

'Fuck!' he shouted. 'You know on second thoughts, I might just come down.' (very similar to Syed on the crane).

I saw him strut over to the fire escape greet my negotiator with a handshake and begin his descent back to ground level. I was stunned. After seven hours of sweet-talking, ego stroking and rationalising, it had only taken a few cardboard boxes to make this lad come to his sentences. Or so I thought.

He came down taking care to watch his step (the irony) and we took him down to the fourth floor of the building where he lived in a small flat with his mum. She was beside herself when we walked through the door, tears streaming down her fat wrinkly cheeks.

I watched as our chap fidgeted around the flat, apologising for the mess he'd made of things. As I was watching him however my instinct began to kick in. *This isn't right,* I thought. *He appears agitated. We should handcuff him and sit him down.*

My brain had barely registered this thought when suddenly, without warning, I saw our chap leap to his feet, run out of the living room and straight to the kitchen. *That's where the knives are kept!* We followed suit as he ran, expecting the worst. But rather than reach for the utensils draw or bread knives, he instead took a running jump at the kitchen window, shattering the glass pane into tiny shards. I wasn't half as quick as my colleague who managed to grab him by the hook of his belt and reel him back in, shards of glass flying in every direction. If he had he managed to go all the way through, he would fallen four floors and broken his neck.

My colleague really did save a life that day, not to mention our careers. I can't help but imagine the headlines if our chap had been successful. *'Police talk suicidal man down from roof only to let him leap to his death in front of his crying mother.'* I would have been the one responsible if it had happened, given that I had failed to instruct my team to restrict the person's movements when he first came down off the roof.

This happens a lot in the world of negotiation. When you've spent hours building rapport with a person, you begin to forget that sometimes more stringent measures are needed. Safety is paramount and we need to remember to put our police heads back on the minute the victim is brought back to safety.

Another mistake I vividly remember, very nearly lost me an eye. This particular incident happened a few years back on yet another suicide intervention. I had been deployed to help a young man who'd locked himself in his house before swallowing numerous tablets and threatening to kill himself. After a few hours the tablets were having little effect, so he'd decided to turn the gas on and put his head in the oven instead. As suicide attempts go, he was trying to tick all the boxes. Annoyingly the only way we could communicate with him was through his locked front door, that I'd been crouched behind for the better part of an hour. I needed better vision into the house to determine whether this young man was really turning on the gas or making a gesture. I decided to open the letter box and take a peek inside. No sooner had I lifted the flap however when I saw a sharp piece of metal shoot straight through towards my face. The bastard had only gone and stuck a sword through the letterbox! I jerked my head back with shock. The blade had been mere centimetres from my eye socket.

This case resulted in a forced entry from our Public Order Shield Team. The pills had begun to take a dangerous effect on our man and he had passed out on the stairwell, mid negotiation. I say it was the tablets but who knows. It's highly likely that I bored him to sleep.

The lesson to take away from two these incidents is that it's impossible to perform this job without making some mistakes. Thankfully, there are always precautions one can take which will ensure that fewer occur. The most salient piece of advice I can offer anyone in this business, is to *trust your instincts* and regularly assess the situation around you. When you are *in the zone*, actively listening, you can forget your own personal safety.

Having knowledge of how to do this job is one thing. Applying it effectively is something else entirely. Innate communication skills, personality, charisma, empathy and above all practice, maketh' the expert negotiator.

In writing this book and entering the dialogue that was recorded, it was interesting to see how many of these incidents ended in tactical solutions or the occurrence of unexpected events. Rarely was success put down to our expert rapport building. As the title of the book states, *'Just when you think you are winning…'* and the words that should follow…*'is the most dangerous time.'* We have at times witnessed a person in a crisis, who is listening to us, responding to our requests, and then they jump, or come out of hiding, point a firearm at armed police and get shot. Never believe it's over until it's over.

I am proud of what I've achieved in my career through negotiating and proud of the capable colleagues I've met along the way. For five years, after retiring from the Met and leaving the world of negotiation behind, I worked for a Crisis and Security department within a risk consultancy firm. There I taught my mystical skills to large corporate clients from across the globe. I trained their staff how to talk to kidnappers and helped them learn how to negotiate the release of their staff if held hostage.

I have been fortunate to work alongside superb crisis management teams, assisting them to manage the return of numerous hostages often for only a few thousand dollars.

I have spoken at public engagements and trained a variety of companies in how to bring kidnap negotiation skills into the workplace. How does this work, you might ask? Remember the description of the average kidnapper? (Driven by ego, showing no remorse, with a destructive but not insane personality. They know right from wrong but choose not to conform to the right. They enjoy controlling others; have a low tolerance for frustration and a need to prove that they can do something worthwhile). Does this sound like anyone you know at your workplace? Odds are you don't like them and building rapport with someone you dislike is very difficult. But here's the thing. Using negotiating skills in the kidnapping world works, because in the end it comes down to listening, influencing and managing people. So why not bring those negotiation skills into the workplace? It's a bit of a no brainer.

I recently left the negotiating world entirely and crossed over into corporate security as a security director for a finance company in Hong Kong. I missed the adrenaline of dealing with serious and life-threatening incidents. Ensuring that people get the right advice when a typhoon 8 is approaching Japan, doesn't provide me with quite the same satisfaction. There were so many weather warnings, I became an Asia weather man for my staff.

But they say you can't keep a good man down, so I have returned to this world and now run my own company and subcontract myself to numerous others. Negotiating and dealing with a crisis is in my blood and always will be. Is this the final chapter? I think not.

Acknowledgements

For all the wonderful sketches that begin each chapter:

James Lythe

James is a natural caricaturist with an interest in portraiture and illustration. A former Irish Guards officer, James is a crisis management consultant for Control Risks and worked with me in London, Munich, Erbil and Pointe-Noire.

For her hard work and patience in editing this publication:

Sophie Burstin

Sophie is an award winning copywriter currently living and working in London.

Her Radio work won her a Bronze Cannes Lion in her first year in the industry. She also won Silver at Campaign Big Awards and 2 Silvers at Creative Circle in 2015.

In her spare time, Sophie is a diligent ghostwriter and writer of short stories.

About the Author

Martin was previously a Chief Superintendent in the Metropolitan Police with an exemplary 30 years' service. He has fifteen years' experience as a Hostage and Crisis Negotiator and Siege Coordinator. Other police roles included; Director of the UK Strategic Firearms Command training. He is experienced in leading civil unrest, public order, firearms, negotiating, surveillance and community teams. A qualified and experienced trainer and assessor in strategic management, security, leadership skills and critical and major incidents.

He has managed and advised clients during live kidnap incidents whilst working as a response consultant as an Associate Director within a global crisis and security consulting company.
Also, in this role he delivered in excess of 200 training programmes in over 40 countries. He designed several new training products that included: kidnap incident management, family liaison, hostage survival, terrorism, siege, and negotiating workshops. Clients included international corporate companies throughout Europe, Asia Pac and the Middle East and Africa. He became a trusted advisor to several major oil and gas clients resulting in an increase of repeated business and company profit margins.

Whilst a senior police leader he deployed as an operational supervisor, managing several post incident police shootings and pan London terrorism incidents. He received numerous Chief Officer Commendations and letters of praise from the head of the United Nations for bravery and managing international kidnap incidents. Martin often performed 24/7 on call responsibility for the UK Metropolitan Police, responsible for authorising the deployment of all firearms officers and hostage and crisis negotiators. As part of a team of negotiators he was successful during high-profile demonstrations at London landmarks including the London Eye, Westminster Abbey and Tower Bridge and has extensive experience dealing with over 100 barricade, hostage and kidnap incidents including being a negotiator during the UK's longest recorded siege.

He has deployed operationally to various countries including, Iraq, Afghanistan, and Israel as lead negotiator and strategic team leader in respect of the kidnapping of British subjects. He was also an advisor to Her Majesty's Ambassadors and the Foreign and Commonwealth Office on international kidnap management.

Printed in Great Britain
by Amazon